IMAGES OF THE SELF

Estelle L. Weinrib

IMAGES OF THE SELF
The Sandplay Therapy Process

Foreword by Dora M. Kalff

SIGO
PRESS

Sigo Press
77 North Washington Street, 201, Boston, Massachusetts 02114

Publisher and General Editor: Sisa Sternback-Scott
Editors: Lindsay Smith, Becky Goodman

Library of Congress Cataloging in Publication Data

Weinrib, Estelle L.
    Images of the self

    Bibliography: p.
    Includes index.
    1. Sandplay——Therapeutic use. 2. Psychotherapy.
3. Child's psychotherapy. 4. Play therapy. 5. Jung, C. G. (Carl
Gustav), 1875–1961. I. Title. Psychoanalytic therapy.
WM [DNLM; 460.6 W424i]
RC489.S25W44 1983   616.89'1653   83–11974
ISBN 0-9384343-19-5
ISBN 0-9384343-16-0 (pbk.)

For Steve, Amy and Ken

CONTENTS

ILLUSTRATIONS

AUTHOR'S NOTE

After many years of a fruitful and rewarding Jungian analysis, I had occasion to spend a summer in the environs of Zurich doing intensive sandplay therapy with Dora M. Kalff. In a short time, a matter of weeks, I reached a previously unexperienced level of my being that moved and astonished me. At first I attributed this to my previous analytical process and development, and to the prodigious personal gifts of Mrs. Kalff. Although intrigued, I was not convinced that sandplay alone could have added such a new dimension. Later, however, after years of study with Kalff, I incorporated sandplay into my analytical practice and found that in itself it accelerates and deepens the therapeutic process. It has proved to be an invaluable therapeutic approach about which not enough is known. This book is an effort to remedy that situation.

I express my profound gratitude to Dora Kalff for her patient teaching and generosity in sharing her thoughts and experiences with me through unnumbered hours. I have the deepest admiration for her creativity and pioneering spirit.

I extend my heartfelt thanks to my patients who have taught me so much, particularly those who have permitted me to use their material: to my caring colleague, Gilda Frantz, without whose intervention this book might never have seen the light of day, and Katherine Bradway for her careful and time-consuming reading of the manuscript, and her invaluable suggestions for improving it; to my friend, Professor Bettina Knapp, for her sensitive guidance through the labyrinthine ways of authorship; to Selma Shapiro whose intelligence and patience in endless typing and retyping were a great comfort; to my loving and always supportive children; and most of all to my incomparable husband—the keeper of the flame. I am a fortunate woman.

E. W.

FOREWORD:

Estelle Weinrib has written a very valuable study on sandplay therapy that helps to understand many important ideas that underlie its practice. She has aptly commented on the practical and theoretical aspects of sandplay and illustrated her experiences with a case. This case shows that sandplay can serve as a powerful medium to reach strong, transformative, inner experiences. From her description one gets the feeling that as a therapist she is able to truly participate in these happenings and to create a favorable space for their arising and transformation. At the same time she is able to offer a consistent and convincing interpretation of the material without ever becoming dogmatic about her views. According to my own experience it is very important when we offer our own interpretation that we leave enough space for the possibility of further suggestions and insights. Because in sandplay we are dealing with a living experience it would be presumptuous to think that it is possible to exhaustively describe it on a conceptual level.

Estelle Weinrib has rightly emphasized the nonverbal character of the process that is occurring through sandplay. It is perhaps possible to say that the healing occurs on what Neumann calls the matriarchal level of consciousness. Although this level of consciousness may be termed matriarchal it does not mean that there is a preponderance of feminine symbolism. The symbolic union of opposites, be it on the abstract level of principles such as sky and earth or be it on a human level of man and woman, is an important feature of the process also on this preverbal level.

I agree with Estelle Weinrib that initially we can talk about a creative regression towards an instinctual level of being. It is also true that the developments occurring after the Self-constellation which lead to a new ego structure are progressive in nature. We have been able to observe that in a nonverbal phase of the process when analytical interpretation is still withheld a positive shift in attitude to the external world and other people can take place. This is the case even when I abstain from a simultaneous analytical discussion of dreams and general behavior patterns. Especially in the beginning phase I prefer to create an open space for the unconscious inner impulses to manifest without the interference of premature conceptualization. When the process has proceeded to a point well after the constellation of the Self, the verbal and analytical work becomes more important. It is at this stage that the unconscious process which has expressed itself in sandplay can be integrated into a conscious appreciation of the changes that have occurred. As I understand it, this phase of elucidation is an integral part of sandplay therapy.

In some cases, people do not wish to talk immediately after the last sandplay picture has been created because of the very depths of the experience they have gone through. They may come back at a later time to look at the pictures and do more analytical work on them.

I have been very impressed by the work of some of my Japanese students which shows very positive nonverbal communication through sandplay resulting in an impressive change in the client. Professor Kawai talks in this context of a transference on the Hara level—a direct communication from one center of a person to the center of the other person. We have to take into account, however, that there exists a considerable difference in the mentality between most of the Western world and the Japanese culture. It is therefore conceivable that a conceptual integration of the experience is more important in our culture than in theirs.

D. M. Kalff

PART I
SANDPLAY THERAPY:
THEORY AND PRACTICE

1. INTRODUCTION

Sandplay is a nonverbal, nonrational form of therapy that reaches a profound preverbal level of the psyche. In this psychotherapeutic modality patients create three-dimensional scenes, pictures or abstract designs in a tray of specific size, using sand, water and a large number of miniature realistic figures.

Unlike the customary practice in verbal dream analysis, interpretations are not offered at the time the pictures are created. Although the patient may associate to the sand pictures as he or she would to a dream, the therapist is receptive but makes minimal comment. Interpretation is delayed until a certain degree of ego stability has been reached. The rationale for this unusual practice and other points made here will be discussed later.

A basic postulate of sandplay therapy is that deep in the unconscious there is an autonomous tendency, given the proper conditions, for the psyche to heal itself.

As a verbal analysis of dreams, personality and life problems is progressing in the direction of enlarged consciousness, the sandplay process encourages a creative *regression* that enables healing. In short, two separate but related processes are occurring, and the interaction between them seems to hasten and enrich the therapeutic endeavor.[1]

Sandplay enables three-dimensional tangible expression of inchoate, unconscious contents. Sand pictures represent figures and landscapes of the inner and outer world, and they appear to mediate between these two worlds and connect them.

Sandplay therapy provides the conditions for a womb-like incubatory period that makes possible the repair of a damaged mother-image which, in turn, enables *constellation* and activation of the *Self*,[2] the subsequent healing of the wounded *ego,* and the recovery of the inner child with all that implies in terms of psychological renewal (see Chapter 5).

[1]At a certain point the sandplay process becomes progressive. This development will be discussed later.
[2]See Glossary for definition of italicized terms.

2. THE EVOLUTION OF SANDPLAY

MAGIC CIRCLES AND FANTASIES

The earliest precursors of sandplay therapy practitioners might be said to be those most primitive tribes who first drew protective magic circles in the earth.

The nearest cultural parallel to sandplay therapy seems to be the sand painting of the Navajo religion wherein ritual sand pictures are used extensively in ceremonies of healing, as well as for divination, exorcism and other purposes.

Pictures are made by chanters or medicine men and initiated assistants who mold and paint symbolic figures of sand on the ground, in prescribed arrangements, enclosed by "guardian" boundaries marked in the sand. The figures represent mythic deities in human or animal form plus natural or geometric symbols, all of which are usually arranged in quadrants around a center, strongly suggesting a *mandala* form, except that the outer boundary (circular, square or rectangular) has an opening to allow evil to get out and good to get in.

These sand paintings can be quite simple or as much as 20 feet in diameter and very elaborate, requiring as many as forty assistants and eight to ten hours to complete. When the painting is finished, the patient or seeker sits on it, while the chanter applies sand from the various figures of the painting to specified parts of the patient's body. All this is to identify the patient with deities represented in the painting. In addition, the sand itself is felt to have healing properties: the patient is said to absorb good from the sand while the sand absorbs evil from him.

The pictures are believed to carry mana and are held sacred:

> To witness the laying of a sand painting may be dangerous for the uninitiated . . . There is, however, a time when even the initiated must not witness the completion of the sand painting preparation, the moment of sanctification when the painting becomes sacred, the instant when the encircling guardian [boundary] of the sand picture is started (Reichard, 1974, p. 160).

The pictures represent blessings only and attract good and repel evil. They are believed to be particularly efficacious in the treatment of trauma, when the patient has been shocked or frightened into unconsciousness (Reichard, p. 681). The sand paintings also "correct symptoms due to contemplation of supernatural things too strong for the patient" (Reichard, p. 717).

The first Jungian to be involved with sandplay therapy might be said to be Jung himself, who described in his autobiography, *Memories, Dreams, Reflections,* how in 1912 he happened upon a healing form of play (Stewart, 1977, pp. 9–11).

After his break with Freud, Jung wrote that he found himself in a painfully confused inner state that yielded neither to analysis of his dreams nor to reexamination of his life. He decided to submit himself to impulses of the unconscious, to do whatever occurred to him. He remembered that as a small boy he had built castles and buildings of stone and mortar made of

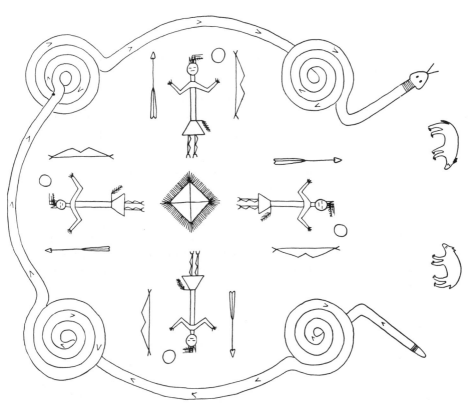

1. Never-ending snake sandpainting.
   A Navaho healing rite.

earth and water. In *Memories, Dreams, Reflections* (1962, p. 174), he writes:

> "The small boy is still around, and possesses a creative life which I lack. But how can I make my way to it?" For as a grown man it seemed impossible to me that I should be able to bridge the distance from the present back to my eleventh year. Yet, if I wanted to re-establish contact with that period, I had no choice but to return to it and take up once more that child life with its childish games. This moment was a turning point in my fate, but I gave in only after endless resistances and with a

sense of resignation. For it was a painfully humiliating experience to realize that there was nothing to be done except play
childish games.

He reports then (*Memories, Dreams, Reflections,* pp. 174–
175) that he played regularly and seriously day after day with
the earth and stones on the edge of the Lake of Zurich:

> In the course of this activity my thoughts clarified, and I was
> able to grasp the fantasies whose presence in myself I dimly felt.
>   Naturally, I thought about the significance of what I was
> doing and asked myself, "Now, really, what are you about?
> You are building a small town, and doing it as if it were a rite!"
> I had no answer to my questions, only the inner certainty that
> I was on the way to discovering my own myth. For the building
> game was only the beginning. It released a stream of fantasies
> which I later carefully wrote down.

The building game, which he continued for some time and
then extended into painting and stone-cutting, released a flow
of fantasies which eventually led to his appreciation of *fantasy*
as "the mother of all possibilities, where, like all psychological
opposites, the inner and outer worlds are joined together in
living union" (*Collected Works* [hereafter cited as *CW*], Vol.
6, p. 52).

Giving concrete form to his own fantasies and his later observation of his patients led him to his discovery of the process
of *individuation,* the *transcendent function,* and the technique of *active imagination.*

PIONEERS IN SANDPLAY THERAPY

Sandplay itself was originated in England by Margaret Lowenfeld who in 1935 published a book about it called *World
Techniques: Play in Childhood.* She attributed the inspiration
for the method to H. G. Wells' book *Floor Games,* published
in 1911.

The method, soon called World Techniques, was used by
Dr. Lowenfeld, a Freudian psychiatrist at the Institute of Child

Psychology in London, and subsequently by clinics in other countries.

In 1956, after attending the Jung Institute for six years, Dora M. Kalff went to a psychiatric conference in Zurich where she was impressed by an exhibition by Dr. Lowenfeld of her World Techniques.[1] Encouraged by Jung, who was her mentor and friend, Kalff left for London to study and work with Lowenfeld and others, including Michael Fordham and D. W. Winnicott. Kalff's experience in London helped clarify for her the direction of her future work.

Returning to Switzerland, she began her practice with children, using Jungian symbology and developing her own version of sandplay therapy. She started with the basic hypothesis postulated by Jung, that there is a fundamental drive toward wholeness and healing in the human psyche. To allow for the healing she decided to give the patient "a free space," to accept him unconditionally, to observe without making judgments and to be guided only by her own observations (Kalff, *Sandplay: A Psychotherapeutic Approach to the Psyche,* 1980). Since she was the only Jungian analyst doing therapy with children in Zurich at that time, there was no one to talk to save Jung himself, who gave her encouragement, advice and such psychological aid and comfort as time allowed.

She used a nonverbal approach, doing nothing to intrude upon the child's process but simply observing and accepting what happened in the hour. She prepared herself for the next hour with the child by trying to assimilate what had happened in the previous one.

The approach here was not unlike Jung's, who in *Memories, Dreams, Reflections* (p. 170) recounts the beginning of his method of dream interpretation:

I felt a necessity to develop a new attitude toward my patients.

[1] The biographical information that follows comes from a personal conversation with Kalff in 1972.

I resolved for the present not to bring any theoretical premises to bear on them, but to wait to see what they would tell me of their own accord. My aim became to leave things to chance.

When the patients spontaneously reported dreams and fantasies, interpretations seemed to follow of their own accord from the patients' replies and associations. I avoided all theoretical points of view and simply helped the patients to understand the dream-images by themselves, without application of rules or theories.

From the beginning, Kalff's patients made rapid and exciting progress. It soon became apparent that an autonomous process was occurring with little or no verbal comment or explanation being given to the child.

Kalff began to recognize stages of development in the sand pictures (to be described later) that were clearly expressions of a psychological maturation occurring within the child. But she had no conceptual frame of reference to explain the phenomena.

After she heard a lecture by Erich Neumann, an eminent Jungian analyst, on his ideas about psychological development in early childhood, Kalff and Neumann had discussions that convinced both of them that her practice was confirming and illustrating some of his theoretical formulations. Neumann, never having practiced therapy with children, had evolved concepts in a purely theoretical way. They planned to do some research together, but Neumann unfortunately died shortly after their meeting.

Kalff then began doing sandplay therapy with adults and discovered that the *same* developmental process occurred as in children, indicating that sandplay operated on a quite primitive level of the unconscious.

Later she met the renowned Zen scholar D. Z. Suzuki and exchanged ideas with him. In Kalff's practice of delaying interpretation, Suzuki saw a parallel with Zen practice, wherein the pupil/seeker-after-wisdom is *not* given a direct answer to his question, but is rather thrown back on his own imagination and inner resources. The meeting with Suzuki reinforced her feeling that her approach was right.

3. A GAME WITHOUT RULES

The basic equipment for sandplay consists of a shallow rectangular sand tray, 28½ inches by 19½ inches, 3 inches deep, and half-filled with sand. The inside of the sand tray is lined with sheet metal or rigid plastic and colored light blue. By moving the sand away from an area at the bottom of the tray, one gets the impression of blue water, which can then serve as a river, lake or ocean. Because of the waterproof lining of metal or plastic, real water can be used to wet the sand so that it can be molded or shaped. Hundreds of miniature figures and small objects are arranged on open shelves and are available for use in making a sand picture. The figures include realistic representations of wild and domesticated animals, fish, birds, shells and craft materials, cars, trains, boats, planes, bridges, buildings, churches, temples, work implements, trees and flowers, human figures (adults and children of many nationalities and races in various walks of life: farmers, workers, soldiers, knights, Eskimos, Africans, Asians, etc.). In short, symbolic objects with which to create a world. The figures should be of good quality so as to appeal to and stimulate the patient's aesthetic and creative sensibilities.

No instructions are given. The patient is simply encouraged to create whatever he or she wishes in the sand tray. The patient may choose to make a landscape or any other kind of picture, or decide to sculpt or just play with the sand. Using the sand tray, the patient is free to play out his fantasies, to externalize and make concrete in three dimensions his inner world.

The therapist sits quietly at a little distance, observes the reactions and behavior of the patient, the development of the picture, and draws a sketch of it to identify the objects in the picture for later study. The patient may or may not speak. He may be perfectly quiet, or he may spontaneously talk about the picture, tell its story, or give some explanation of what he is doing, and what the objects mean to him. Often something in the picture moves the patient to speak of personal memories or present concerns. Sometimes, after reacting to the picture, he may decide to change it, which he is free to do, and one can see that a development has occurred, perhaps just by virtue of his having created the picture and having reacted to it.

The mere making of the picture seems to have a good effect. Deeply *introverted* and particularly tense patients tend to relax. Hyperactive or hysterical patients tend to quiet down, as though touching concrete, three-dimensional reality has a calming effect in itself. It is particularly effective in reaching patients who tend to oververbalize, rationalize, or intellectualize and, of course, the opposite kind of patients—those who have trouble verbalizing at all. *Intuitives* benefit from the concreteness of the process, which tends to slow them down and "ground" them.[1] The therapist listens, observes and participates empathically and cognitively, with as little verbalization as possible.

[1]Instances where sandplay is neither effective nor suitable are discussed later.

2. Sandplay figures.

After the picture is finished, the therapist may ask the patient to tell the story of the picture, or may ask relevant questions or elicit the patient's comments and associations regarding the pictures, or speak of matters suggested by them. Starting with those comments and associations that are readily forthcoming from the patient, the therapist evaluates the picture in the light of Jungian symbology and any *archetypal* amplifications that suggest themselves.

The therapist does not offer this information at this time, does not press for associations or confront the patient in any way. Interpretations can imply value judgments—or they can be inferred.[2] The aim of sandplay is to offer really free play, devoid of rules and in safe circumstances. It offers an opportunity for being and doing without encumbrances. To press for associations would be to encourage cerebral activity, which is not desirable here except in its most spontaneous exercise. Pressing for associations would encourage cerebral verbal discussion and the expectation of response from the therapist.

(I make occasional exceptions to this practice. If the patient does not enjoy doing sandplay and is skeptical of its value, I comment on some aspect of the early picture to assure him that his pictures are, in fact, communicating his unspoken feelings, plus other information that is helpful. There are other exceptions: If a particular theme has urgent significance; or if a patient is acutely anxious and needs the reassurance of cognitive understanding.)

The therapist is, of course, free to use any ideas he or she has derived from the sandplay process in an indirect way in the verbal analysis. In fact, the patient's response to the introduction of these ideas provides one way to check on the validity of the analyst's "reading" of the pictures.

A sand picture is never dismantled in the patient's presence. When the patient leaves, his picture intact, an imprint is left

[2]A more detailed conceptual rationale for delaying interpretation is offered later.

in his mind out of which something new can evolve. Not infrequently patients report carrying the image with them, finding
it comforting. Sometimes they change the image in their mind's
eye. Sometimes they plan their next picture with the previous
one in mind.

To destroy a picture in the patient's presence would be to
devalue a completed creation, to break the connection between
the patient and his inner self, and the unspoken connection
to the therapist.

Photographic slides are taken of the picture after the patient
leaves. At the end of a series of pictures, when the ego has
become strong enough to integrate the material properly, or
when mutually agreed upon, the therapist projects the slides
for the patient. At this time, explanations, amplifications and
interpretations may be given and questions are answered. Often
little needs to be said even then, for the slides themselves seem
to speak directly to the patient, as he literally sees pictures of
his own developmental process. In a sense, then, the sandplay
process may be likened to a prolonged dream or active imagination that needs to work itself out.

Jung did something similar when dealing with the dream
material in *Psychology and Alchemy* (*CW,* vol. 12). In regard
to this approach Jung said:

> The intellect has no objection to "analyzing" the unconscious
> as a passive object; on the contrary, such an activity would
> coincide with our rational expectations. But to let the uncon-
> scious go its own way and to experience it as a reality is some-
> thing that exceeds the courage and capacity of the average . . .
> [person] (p. 52).
>   . . . the doctor . . . who tries to correct the mysterious and
> well-nigh inscrutable workings of nature with his so-called
> scientific attitude is merely putting his shallow sophistry in
> place of nature's healing processes . . . (p. 223).

In sandplay, no interpretation is offered until the process is
completed and the slides are shown, because the therapist has

been using insights garnered from the sand pictures in the analytical sessions just as ideas gained analytically shed light on the meaning of the pictures.

The value of the retrospective slide showing, however, is manifold. It helps make the experience with the unconscious more concrete. It reiterates and reinforces change. The impact on the patient can effect further change. Sometimes patients want the slides shown to their partners in a relationship. The partner may also be affected, as though the unconscious of the patient speaks to the partner.

The slide presentation offers another dimension of the therapeutic experience in that the patient is able to see with his own eyes where he has been and what he has literally created.

At the slide presentation the therapist can help the patient make connections between the visual images and the happenings of his inner and outer life. Often the patients spontaneously recognize the connections between the symbolic meanings of the pictures and themselves, which reinforces their sense of competence. Frequently, new insights are garnered by both therapist and patient as they sit together studying the slides. Sometimes the patient sees connections the therapist has missed.

The slide showing is, by its very nature, an occasion for reinforcement of the patient's ego. It is, after all, a show for and about him, created by him. It is decidedly not the time for the therapist to demonstrate his "rich" knowledge of the archetypes or his "brilliant" creativity.

In general, the amount of interpretive or archetypal amplificatory information offered to the patient at the slide showing (as with dream interpretation in the analytical process) depends on the readiness of the ego to absorb it, and the interest and capacity of the patient to understand it.

Occasionally a patient is not particularly interested in seeing the slides. It is as though the creation of the pictures had been an enactment in itself that closed the *gestalt*. The patient is already beyond that period of his life. It is simply over and not important anymore.

On the other hand, the slide presentation can be moving, exciting or just plain fun. It can also have an *inflationary* effect. The therapist should be sensitive to all of the above issues and to the possibility that he and the patient may be looking at the patient's soul pictures.

Because so little is said by the therapist during the sandplay process, it is particularly important that he choose his words sensitively. Recognizing that premature intervention by him in the process, except under unusual circumstances, might disturb what is conceived to be an essentially unconscious healing process, the sandplay therapist must discipline his urge to find ready answers to unclear questions.

Because he does not immediately share his impression of the sand pictures and receives no direct modifying feedback from the patient, the therapist must clearly understand that any evaluations, interpretations, or amplifications he makes about the pictures are merely hypotheses that are subject at any time to modification or rejection. Clearly, an interpretation or amplification made without direct associations or corrective or corroborative response from the patient can provide only a provisional frame of reference.

Any symbol can have many meanings. Therefore, it is advisable that the therapist have a relatively wide knowledge of symbology from which to choose interpretations. However, the specific interpretation of a particular symbol may be less important than the process itself and the relationship between himself and the patient. It is, of course, imperative that the therapist's ideas about the patient and the pictures are in the right general direction with regard to the archetypal and diagnostic issues.

The therapist needs to check rigorously any interpretation or hypothesis he may infer, against the reality of the patient's life, his attitudes and behavior. Otherwise there is danger of the therapist going off into his own archetypal magical fantasy tour or intellectual gambit, both of which may have little or nothing to do with either the psyche or workaday life of the patient.

The possible hazards inherent in delayed interpretation notwithstanding, sandplay brings to the therapeutic process the element of genuinely free play, with all that it implies in terms of freedom and creativity. Sandplay is not a game with rules. It is free and encourages playfulness. Its value lies in its experiential noncerebral character.

4. EIGHT BASIC CONCEPTS

Sandplay therapy as developed by Kalff rests, to a large extent, on the theoretical constructs of C. G. Jung and Erich Neumann. Eight concepts relevant to this method will be discussed in this chapter: others are described in Chapters 5, 6 and 7. I also venture ideas of my own.

1. Psychological development of the individual is archetypally determined and under normal circumstances is similar for everyone (Neumann, 1954).

2. The psyche consists of consciousness and the unconscious and the interaction between them, and is a teleologically oriented self-regulatory system. It contains a drive toward wholeness and has a tendency to balance itself through the compensatory function of the unconscious.[1] The drive to reali-

---

[1]Compensation implies here that there is a relationship between the unconscious and the conscious mind wherein a content missing from consciousness and required for wholeness of the personality will appear in accentuated form in the unconscious, making itself known through a dream or powerful affect deriving from an activated complex.

zation and wholeness (the Self) suggests that the psyche, like the body, under adequate circumstances has a tendency to heal itself (Jung, "On the Nature of the Psyche," *CW*, Vol. 8, pp. 159–234).

3. The Self is the totality (conscious and unconscious) of the personality and its directing center. It is the central organizing factor of the psyche out of which the ego, which is only the center of consciousness, evolves. Jung states: "The ego stands to the Self as the moved to the mover, or as object to subject . . . The Self, like the unconscious, is an a priori existent out of which the ego evolves. It is, so to speak, an unconscious prefiguration of the ego" (*CW*, Vol. 11, p. 259 par. 391).

As modern consciousness evolved, the ego gained preponderance over the Self, particularly in Western intellectual development. The primacy of the intellect has resulted in an unbalanced, overly rational personality that is peculiarly subject to neuroses. The autonomy of the ego is limited since the ego's roots are in the unconscious. The ego is vulnerable to influence by emotionally charged *complexes* acting in a compensatory way. The more the ego tries to suppress or ignore an activated complex, the more the complex will rob the ego of control. (Despite assertion of conscious will, who among us has not overreacted to a situation in which a complex has been stirred?) A primary aim of Jungian analysis and sandplay therapy is "to relativize the ego"—that is, for the ego to relinquish its illusory dominance and to reestablish a connection and continuing relationship between consciousness and the unconscious.

4. Jung's reinterpretation of the incest theory suggests that: as the mother is the source of physical life, so the unconscious is the source of psychological life. The mother and the unconscious, therefore, can be seen as symbolic feminine equivalents. The drive to return to the mother can be seen as a drive to return to the unconscious. Under certain circumstances, this may be regressive, leading to neurosis and psychosis; psycho-

logical illness or death. In other circumstances, that is, in the individuation process, the regression may be temporary and in service of psychological renewal and symbolic rebirth (*CW,* Vol. 5, Part II, p. 235).

After a degree of maturity (i.e., ego development and separation from the personal mother) has been achieved, Jung sees the drive to reconnect with the symbolic mother (the unconscious) as necessary in the individuation process. Indeed, separation from the unconscious and reconnection and continuing relationship to it are aims of Jungian analysis and are the essence of the individuation process. During the psychotherapeutic process, separation and reconnection may, and do, go on simultaneously.

5. In my view, psychological healing and expansion of consciousness, though related, are *not* identical.[2] Healing implies first that there has been a wounding and possible impairment of natural organic function, and second, that the wound has then been remedied and natural functioning has been restored. Consciousness implies awareness of what one is feeling, thinking and doing and the capacity to make choices in one's action and communications that are relatively free of control by complexes.

In short, psychological healing involves restoration of the capacity to function normally, while ego-consciousness has to do with awareness and choice of what we are doing while we function. Expanded consciousness, while it may contribute to healing, does not ensure it. On the other hand, healing, by restoring the psyche to its natural functioning, creates a condition out of which the insight and consciousness that are natural

[2]Kalff suggested that there was a difference between consciousness and healing when she said in a conversation in 1972: "Rational consciousness in the process is not necessary. It is similar to the idea in the East that all is consciousness. There is a content that is simply not verbalized or conceptualized. Somewhere a person knows. We don't necessarily have to make something conscious that is unconscious in order to heal."

to the human personality will evolve organically (Weinrib, 1983).

6. Psychological healing, in this context, is an emotional, nonrational phenomenon that takes place on the matriarchal level of consciousness hypothesized by Erich Neumann (see later in this chapter) and which Kalff calls the preverbal level. Healing at this level enables renewal of the personality and expansion of consciousness.

7. Both healing *and* the expansion of consciousness are desirable ends in psychotherapy. I believe that the use of sandplay deepens and accelerates the therapeutic endeavor because two processes are occurring, the processes being intimately related yet separate. During the same period that a verbal analysis of complexes, dreams, personality and life problems is progressing in a thrust toward consciousness, sandplay encourages a creative regression[3] that enables healing precisely because of delayed interpretation and the deliberate discouragement of directed thinking.

In practice, the two processes appear to interrelate and complement each other. Although patients may depict dream images in the sand tray, very often certain images or themes appear in the sand tray *before* they appear in dreams. Perhaps this is so because the making of a sand picture is an enactment in sensate reality, a concrete action that stimulates archetypal activity, which then manifests in dreams (or perhaps directly into changing attitudes and behavior) (Weinrib, 1983).

For example, if the image of a bridge connecting two entities appears in a dream, the bridge is a symbol of connection. However, in sandplay, the patient has actually placed a bridge that in fact connects two separate parts. And that physical fact *may*

---

[3]After the constellation of the Self and the emergence of a renewed and strengthened ego, the sandplay process takes on a more verbal and progressive character. The patient is then more capable of relating independently to the inner being and the outer world.

have an effect on the unconscious, whatever the dynamics may be.

8. The natural healing process can be effectively activated by therapeutic play and stimulation of creative impulses via conditions provided by the "free and protected space" as propounded by Kalff. The Jungian view of the function of the symbol is that it is a healing agent that acts as a reconciling bridge between opposites; that it "can be regarded as an attempt of the unconscious to lead regressive *libido* into a creative act, thus pointing the way to a resolution of the conflict" (Harding, 1961, p. 8).

I believe that the making of a sand picture is in itself a symbolic and creative act. Provided it is happening within the free and protected space (see Chapter 5), symbolic active fantasizing by the patient stimulates the imagination, freeing neurotically fixated energy and moving it into creative channels, which in itself can be healing.

The making of sand pictures by the patient is voluntary. Pictures are not necessarily made at every meeting. Sometimes weeks, more rarely even months, go by between the making of sand pictures because the image, coming out of the depths of the psyche and concretized in a creative act, needs to develop and move on in its own time. When no pictures are made, a regular Jungian verbal analysis proceeds, including the interpretation of dreams, work on *typological* problems, interpersonal relations, and other issues. In the verbal analytical process, etiological and teleological insight and the expansion of consciousness are the goals. Symbolic material emerging from the unconscious and the stuff of everyday life is integrated into consciousness as soon as possible. In sandplay—a ruminative, contemplative process—understanding is less important than the healing process itself.

With regard to healing, Jung likened the compensatory healing tendency of the psyche to that of the body as early as 1920, when he said: "Just as the body reacts in a purposeful manner to injuries, infections or abnormal ways of life, so do the psychic functions react with purposeful defense mechanisms to unnatural or dangerous disturbances" ("General Aspects of the Psychology of the Dream," *Spring,* 1956, p. 4).

The natures of psychological healing and consciousness remain at heart mysteries. We can only conjecture about them and recognize that healing is not identical with consciousness as we tend to think of consciousness: that is, as an accretion of ego awareness. If ego-consciousness were all, insight and awareness could be relied upon to change our emotional responses and behavior, but all too often they do not.

It seems to me that, to a large extent, the function of expanded ego-consciousness is to offer us choices of attitudinal or behavioral response to our autonomous instinct-based emotional states, which in spite of our best efforts remain quite independent of our will: nor would we wish to rid ourselves of feeling and emotional reactions because they lend depth, color and intensity to existence. They are the very stuff of life.

Neumann offers a plausible hypothesis for nonverbal, nonrational psychological healing, postulating two kinds of consciousness. He defines ego-consciousness (with which we are all familiar) as relatively autonomous, characterized by reason, judgment and order. He suggests that ego-consciousness, as we know it, evolved from a layer of the psyche he calls patriarchal, which was a late development in all mankind and which exists in women as well as men. He suggests that a second consciousness, called *matriarchal consciousness,* is rooted in a much deeper, earlier and more archaic level of the psyche and that it too exists in all of us, male or female (Neumann, 1954).

Neumann describes this matriarchal mode of consciousness as a half-conscious process in which there is no willed ego-intention. It is subject to the unconscious and reflects unconscious processes, yet carries qualities of awareness, nonverbal comprehension, contemplation, conception, circumambulation, realization and bringing forth: a kind of psychological state of incubation or pregnancy. I believe all of the above are precisely the qualities of experience in sandplay, which tends to support the notion that sandplay does indeed operate at the matriarchal level and that healing occurs there.

Neumann goes on to describe matriarchal consciousness as an observing awareness and attentiveness, rather than directed thought or judgment, and notes that it is affected by feeling and *intuition*. Its function with regard to patriarchal consciousness is to focus libido on a particular psychic event, intensifying its effect until it reaches consciousness. The patriarchal head-ego then uses the experience as a basis for action, or the formulation of abstract conclusions and the expansion of consciousness.

Neumann (1954a, pp. 91–92) also suggests that on the matriarchal level of consciousness lies healing:

> It is the regenerating power . . . that, in nocturnal darkness or by the light of the moon, performs its task, a mysterium in a mysterium, from out of itself, out of nature, with no aid from the head ego.
>
> . . . it is (in) the *darkness* where recovery takes place, and also those events in the soul which in obscurity, by processes only the heart can know, allow men to "outgrow" their insoluble crises.

Also particularly relevant to sandplay therapy and its healing properties is Neumann's formulation regarding ego-development: The early constellation and activation of the Self between birth and the third year of life is a prerequisite for the development of a healthy ego (Neumann, 1966, pp. 81–106; 1973, p. 13ff.) Although the Self is present at birth, its evolution as a positive force is dependent on an uninterrupted emotional and physical closeness between mother (or mother surrogate) and child, which he calls the mother-child unity. This undisturbed mother-child bonding is particularly crucial during the first year of life while the child is in what Neumann calls a post-uterine *uroboric* state, in which the Self of the child is still symbiotically contained in the mother. Any disruption in the mother-child unity disturbs the normal and timely separation of the Self of the child from that of the mother and results in the development of a wounded, dependent, needy ego between the ages of one and four; this impaired ego condition can persist for a lifetime.

The needy ego with insufficient inner support from the organizing and regulating force of the Self is prey to narcissism, neurosis and psychosis. Only with a positively activated Self can there be sufficient inner support to enable development of an authentic ego capable of psychological separation from the mother (and also the father), and the establishment of an adequate and individual relationship to both the inner and outer worlds.

The needy ego feels overwhelmed by environmental pressures and may react in any of several ways. It may take an overly introverted route, withdrawing into fantasy and in danger of being overwhelmed by the unconscious. Or, it may lose any sense of inner self by making an excessively extraverted adjustment, by acceding to pressures to perform, to be good, etc. I am reminded of one patient who referred to herself as "a dancing bear" and another who called himself "a song and dance kid." In some cases, the primary adaptive *function* is grossly overdeveloped at the expense of the other functions, or the weak ego may make a totally false adjustment by adopting any function that lends itself to environmental acceptance. This often occurs with *feeling* types who adopt *thinking* as their primary function.

Through its noninterpretive, nonverbal technique sandplay encourages the reconstitution of a psychological mother-child unity, enabling the constellation of the Self and leading to the development of a stronger ego. It encourages a therapeutic regression to the matriarchal level, to what Goethe characterized as the "realm of the Mothers," where psychological healing and renewal can take place.

5. A FREE AND PROTECTED SPACE

> The free and protected space is the necessary security space. Like mountain climbing, where one doesn't leave one foothold or take another step until one has a clear idea of where to take the next step and has secured oneself with rope or hand before taking the next step. In this case, the guide or rope is the therapist.—Dora Kalff (conversation, August 1973)

Central to Kalff's sandplay therapy is the concept of the "free and protected space" which has both physical and psychological dimensions.

The physical element of the free and protected space is, of course, the concrete nature of sandplay. The idea of protection implies the limitation of freedom. The nature of sandplay in itself offers freedom and protection (limitation). While one is free to create whatever one wishes, the number of figures, though extensive, is still finite, so that the fantasy of the patient is held within safe bounds. Since the physical dimensions of the sand tray are limited and containing, in that the entire area can be seen at a glance without moving the eyes or head, the tray has the effect of focusing and then reflecting back the inner vision. The three-dimensional, realistic figures give form to still inchoate inner images. If we assume that archetypes are the forming forces in the background of the phenomenal world, then behind every miniature figure lies an archetype. The figures, then, serve to incarnate archetypal images in a manageable size and shape in a protected environment.

Psychological shelter is provided by the protected atmosphere of the therapeutic situation. The patient is given *really* unconditional acceptance in that there is no confrontation, no intellectualization or interpretation.

The aim is to provide a maternal space or psychological womb, an emotional metaphor for the uroboric mother-child unit. In this safe "space," healing of the inner psychological wound can occur, the Self can be constellated and the inner child rediscovered, with all of its potentiality for creativity and renewal.

Any introduction of thinking into this womb-like space would disturb if not destroy the process, as would the premature breaching of the vessel in an alchemical process. Therefore, it is best to avoid interpreting sand pictures at least until after the Self has been constellated and the renewed ego, now relating to and in turn supported by the Self, emerges.

Interpretations offered *after* such a development can be heard and absorbed in a different way because an inner sense of security has coalesced. Then one can relate from one's inner self to what is heard from outside. Then, there is less chance of being unduly influenced by the therapist and less need for defensive rejection of new insights.

In general, the role of the sandplay therapist is to listen, observe and participate empathically. However, it should be emphasized that the success of the endeavor depends not only on the therapist's cognitive understanding of the symbolic meaning of the picture, but his familiarity with the developmental stages in the process reflected in the pictures. These stages include: At least partial resolution of key complexes; a manifestation of totality and with it an experience or intimation of suprapersonal numinosity that usually accompanies a constellation of the Self, the emergence of a differentiated contrasexual element (*animus/anima*); and a new ego attitude with regard to the transpersonal and to daily life. Kalff calls this the emergence of a "relativized ego" capable of relating productively to both the inner and outer worlds.

Experience has shown that without understanding on the part of the therapist of these stages and their symbolic representations, the process is only minimally effective. This understanding enables an unspoken rapport between therapist and patient, a mother-child bond, for through the concrete images in the pictures, the therapist knows consciously what the patient knows unconsciously.

Essentially, the emotional and psychological free and protected space is provided by the personality of the therapist as the psychological container and protector of the process.

To forgo any immediate knowledge of the meaning of the pictures or any insight into what is happening to him, the patient must trust the therapist, who must be worthy of that trust in every way. He should have had a deep analysis himself and adequate clinical training, including extensive knowledge of archetypal symbolism. He should have had a meaningful personal experience doing sandplay as a patient himself. He should be familiar with the stages of development as they manifest in the process, and he should have studied and compared many sand pictures, which is the only way to learn to read them. As the carrier of the process, he should have achieved rootedness in himself.

It would be an unfortunate misunderstanding to believe all one needs is a tray with some sand, a collection of small objects and a dictionary of symbols. Just companioning a patient while he makes pictures will not accomplish much, nor will interpreting pictures as though they were dreams.

One can, of course, do either or both, but the effects will not
be the same.

Critical is the ability of the therapist to assimilate the feeling
and atmosphere of the process and the individual pictures.
In an emotional sense the therapist "enters" the sand tray with
the patient and participates empathically in the act of creation,
thus establishing a profound and wordless rapport. The silent
capacity to enter into the creation of his world with the patient
can, in itself, help repair the feeling of isolation with which
so many people are afflicted.

Since the empathic participation of the therapist is so important, I reiterate that the therapist should have had a deep personal encounter with sandplay so that he can have some personal feeling for the nature of the process. This therapeutic
mode produces a different kind of experience than a verbal
analysis. Therefore, it should have been lived by the therapist
if the hoped-for bonding is to occur.

Perhaps some comments of one cerebral patient who had
difficulty gaining access to his feelings, and who was particularly drawn to sandplay, may give some further indication of
the sensitivity required by the sandplay therapist:

*When you're talking in a session, you can lie to yourself
without even knowing it. You forget part of a dream or leave
out important things, sometimes consciously.*

*You do the same at the beginning of sandplay because you
want to make an impression. But because you are actually
doing something physically—reaching out voluntarily with
your hands—somehow you know when you are fooling someone. You know when it's phony, when you are cheating.
Sometimes you have to cheat because you're not ready, even
if you don't know why.*

*You choose an object, you put it back. You become more
aware of a feeling. The tray becomes an extension of yourself.
I know what feels right to put into it. If it doesn't* feel *right,*

I take it out. It makes my feelings accessible to me, helps me to distinguish them.

It tells me I have a feeling—whether I'm celebrating a something or a nothing.

I know how I feel when I make a picture. It tells me.

It's like an unspoken dialogue between me and myself. Sometimes I'd just as soon no one else was present. There are things I'm not ready to share.

6. RECONSTRUCTING THE MOTHER IMAGE

What has been spoiled by a father can only be made good by
a father, just as what has been spoiled by the mother can only
be repaired by a mother.—Jung, *CW,* Vol. 14, p. 182.

Basic to Jungian theory is the idea that the archetypes are
manifested through images that are evoked by an individual's
life experience. When insufficient parenting and/or mothering
has occurred, the image of the mother is injured and is not
adequate to serve its protective, nurturing function. The injured
inner-image skews the individual's perception and response
and hampers normal maturation of the personality.

Esther Harding, in *The Parental Image* (1965, p. 39), suggests that the archetypal mother-image we all carry is subject
to two kinds of damage. The first, the natural injury, occurs
inevitably when the primordial identity with the mother is
breached in the normal thrust toward consciousness and separation, because any increase in consciousness entails injury to

the primal uroboric archetypal image itself. The connection with wholeness is lost. However, when there has been sufficient mothering, the maternal image is adequate to serve as mediator between the individual and the archetypal power that stands behind the image. The ego is protected then and the personality can develop normally.

According to Harding, this natural injury is the *sine qua non* in the evolution of human consciousness. It can later be healed in the individual when the adult ego, at the appropriate time, reestablishes contact and a continuing dialogue with the maternal unconscious and the Self in the individuation process. Then "the unconscious becomes the source of life and light as the parents, particularly the personal mother, has been" (Harding, p. 30).

The second possible injury to the maternal image is pathological and occurs when there is early maternal deprivation that produces serious injury to the archetypal image of the mother:

> . . . such children suffer in conscious development and in the unconscious the image of the parent that they encounter is of a negative and destructive mother. It is as if for them, the earliest image of the maternal has been injured. The very pattern of "mother" is distorted, it is hostile instead of friendly, cruel instead of kind, death-dealing instead of life-giving. Children who have suffered in this way live in a pathological inner state, for the relation of a child to his mother is of paramount importance in his development as an individual, and when this is negative the child's growth is dwarfed and distorted (Harding, pp. 10–11).

In that case, Harding says (p. 19), "there is no chance of a real cure unless the injured archetypal image can itself be reconstructed." She goes on to say, "The injured imago has first to be dissolved so that the archetypal image of wholeness . . . can be restored in its healthful aspect."

This can usually be achieved by the emergence of a positive image that can be evoked by a positive emotional experience with a mother surrogate. For even if experience of the image has been negative, Harding (p. 152) maintains, "Deep in the unconscious lies the image of the archetypal parent (mother) in its nurturing and protective aspect together with the corresponding longing of the child to be loved and cared for."

On the assumption that early maternal deprivation results in an injury to the archetypal mother image which severely hampers development of the ego, sandplay therapy attempts to repair damage to the archetypal mother image by metaphorically reconstructing the disturbed uroboric mother-child unity, which enables the positive constellation of the Self, restoration of the natural functioning of the psychic system, and the consequent emergence of an effective ego.

7. RECOVERY OF THE FEMININE

The efficacy of sandplay is not limited to cases of maternal deprivation, although it is particularly effective in such cases. The primary thrust of sandplay is the reestablishment of access to the feminine elements of the psyche in both men and women, elements that have been repressed in Western Judeo-Christian culture.

In instances of paternal domination, as in the case presented in Part II of this book, the key is recovery of the feminine in a young man who had been totally identified with his patriarchal father and controlled by him. But even where there has been adequate mothering, social and cultural pressures have served to repress the feminine.

As used in this work, the term *feminine* is not limited to the female gender. The Jungian view is that all of us are to some extent androgynous. Just as we all have male and female hormones, so we carry contrasexual psychological characteristics; different modes of perceiving, thinking, acting, reacting and relating.

For those who object to using the terms masculine and feminine, one could as easily use the Eastern Asian terms of Yang and Yin, or Logos and Eros, or A and B. The point is to indicate that there are, in everyday reality, two distinctly different modes of relating and functioning. In myths, legends and in modern people's dreams the two modes are generally represented by either masculine or feminine symbols. The feminine qualities in men are personified by the term *anima*. In women, the masculine counterpart is called the *animus*.

FEMININE ASPECTS OF SANDPLAY

The feminine principle is composed of drive elements which are related to life as life, as an unpremeditated spontaneous, natural phenomenon, to the life of the instincts, the life of the flesh, the life of concreteness, of earth, of emotionality; directed toward people and things" (E. C. Whitmount, 1969, p. 189).

Sandplay therapy in its concrete, spontaneous and emotional aspects has peculiarly feminine characteristics. The patient actually engages physically with the sand which is considered an element of the earth, the quintessential feminine element. Earth, like woman, bears life and nutrition.

Tangible, three-dimensional figures and materials are used in an enclosed, physical area of specific dimensions, employed only for a particular purpose at a fixed time. Sandplay, then, takes on a kind of ritualistic aura. The sand tray becomes a metaphorical temenos, or sacred ground, where a physical symbolic ritual enactment takes place that is reminiscent of the ceremonies and atmosphere of the early mystery religions. While patients may begin the process with some diffidence, skepticism, condescension or embarrassment, more often than not an atmosphere of absorption, concentration and seriousness develops that is appropriate to a ritual enactment.

Since there is no interpretation during sandplay itself, there is clearly an experiential rather than ideational emphasis, and a feminine acceptance of "what is" since there are no rules and no "right" way to play.

The patience and care required to create the physical reality of the sand pictures are the same qualities necessary in the traditional tasks of spinning and weaving or kneading. Patience fosters connection and relatedness.

> In the process of painstakingly making pictures, one learns the patience to let things grow. In doing the pictures something grows within. It is advisable that there be time between the making of pictures, to let what is growing solidify. When one has learned patience, one has tolerance for others (Kalff, conversation, August 1973).

One creates a concrete symbolic representation of one's inner world. The translation of inner fantasy into three-dimensional reality with everyday figures helps to limit, to fix and concretize fantasy which is, by its very nature, limitless and amorphous. Sandplay, then, offers a transitional step away from what can be the siren song of the unconscious and toward the "as isness" of the world of everyday people and things, the reality with which we all need to deal.

The concreteness of sandplay offers a dimension different from either drawing, or sculpting, or active imagination, which are traditional Jungian forms of interacting with internal images. An advantage of sandplay is that it requires no skill at all. It offers immediate three-dimensional entry into the playworld of childhood. Drawing, while a physical activity, is exercised on a horizontal, two-dimensional plane. Sculpting, while three-dimensional, requires at least manual dexterity, if not skill, and does not provide the boundaries of the sand tray. Active imagination, effective as it is, is a purely mental activity; sandplay therapy is, in fact, a kind of concrete active imagination.

A FEMININE WAY TO THE SPIRIT

> When the spirit is unrelated to the body, it manifests itself in its negative aspect. The over-endowment of the intellect ham-

pers human development because it leads to suppression of feeling and contempt for the body. Contempt for the body is expressed either in repression or unlimited license (Kalff, conversation, August 1973).

The appearance of symbols of totality in their sand pictures, and the patients' deeply felt numinous experiences, led Kalff to the idea that sandplay is a way to the spirit.

Her early work with Jung and her study of Asian thought with its inclusion of the feminine principle (Yin) as an active element in religious disciplines, all contributed to her early certainty of the necessity of a feminine mode in religious experience and creative endeavor, that there existed an intimate connection between the feminine and creativity and the spirit.

She began to see the feminine as a source of creativity and meaning. In her practice she saw that in the sand something activated by the mind brought forth a concrete creation which in the intuitive way of women brought forth insight, wisdom and *numinous* experience. Relativization of the ego (see p. 77) via encounter with the Self was experienced as numinous and was expressed in unmistakably religious symbols. In her practice she also saw that access to the spirit was achieved by women through reaching the profoundest levels of their feminine beings, and by men through their relationship to the feminine within themselves. This relationship, paradoxically, reinforced men's masculine sense of themselves because they felt more secure and whole.

Kalff began to believe that the material elements of sandplay acted as a kind of a metaphor for the body. She found confirmation for this hypothesis when patients who were physically ill unconsciously made pictorial representations in the sand of diseased organs whose shape they did not know; or there would be some representation of the location in the body where the organ was situated (Seminar at the University of California in Santa Cruz, March 1979). At the very least, sandplay acted as a nonverbal mediator between the inner impulse and outer reality. She saw that working in the sand or earth was in itself a feminine activity:

> Digging with our hands we are actively working in the earth, digging out the energies of the feminine . . . This feminine activity may give immediate access to the deepest transcendental stratum. Reactivation of the feminine may be a way to reactivate the spirit. Centuries of neglect of feminine reality has led to the dessication of spirit; rigidity and dogma. Our deepest religious impulses have been thwarted (Kalff, conversation, August 1973).

Ann Belford Ulanov, in her book *The Feminine in Jungian Psychology and in Christian Theology*, expresses ideas similar to those Kalff evolved through her practice. Ulanov points out (p. 169) that spiritual perception and apperception are in themselves feminine functions since they depend on what Neumann called an *einfall*, a sudden irrational, emotional insight, which is characterized as "the thrusting of spiritual contents 'into consciousness with sufficient force to fascinate and control it' . . . the ego *receives* its spiritual contents into itself. The ego does not so much create the spiritual contents as it is created by them."

Ulanov goes on to say (p. 173): "It is also the feminine quality of activity, with its readiness to receive and respond with the whole being, that is essential in religious experience."

Her description of feminine ego activity describes precisely the kind of activity involved in sandplay (pp. 172–173):

> The quality of feminine ego activity is to accept a conception, to carry knowledge, to assimilate it, and to allow it to ripen. *It is a way of submitting to a process,* which is seen as simply happening and is not to be forced or achieved by an effort of the will . . . (it) is a mixture of attentiveness and contemplation.

Ulanov (p. 170) characterizes feminine understanding as generally concerned with "meaning rather than with facts or ideas, with organic rather than with mechanical processes or

chains of causation." Quoting Neumann, she speaks of feminine understanding as nonverbal comprehension, circumambulation, and conception, which are precisely the qualities of
experience in sandplay therapy.

In describing the feminine mode of experience (p. 172),
Ulanov might well be describing the experience of sandplay
therapy when she says:

> The knowledge that results from this kind of growth process is
> comprehension rather than intellection or information about
> something. Because this kind of knowing involves participation
> of the whole personality and affects concrete changes in it, the
> comprehension has a concrete rather than abstract quality.
> Such knowledge cannot be imparted, proved or even accounted
> for. The inner experience behind it is scarcely able to be com-
> municated verbally. We have all found ourselves saying about
> such understanding, "If you haven't had the experience, I can't
> explain it to you."

8. SANDPLAY AS A WAY
TO TRANSFORMATION

Precisely because the collective unconscious is so vast, there is
a need for sensation reality, three-dimensions, and the confine-
ment of the box. It provides containment and security. It contains the fantasies. The energies, contained, yet able to move,
are more readily transformed (Kalff, conversation, June 1972).

One of the most frequently used words in the Jungian lexi-
con is transformation. According to *Webster's New International Dictionary,* to transform "implies a thorough and
radical change whether in appearance or nature." Psychological transformation would include, I suspect, subjective and
objective changes in a person: apperceptions, attitudes, value
systems, behavior, self-image, perception of the inner and
outer worlds; who one is in relation to oneself, others, society
and the transpersonal; a feeling of rebirth. These and other
definitions notwithstanding, it seems to me that the process
of psychological transformation remains a mystery.

All we can do is describe the phenomena we see clinically
and the circumstances under which they occur. How psychological transformation happens remains a mystery because it
is an unconscious process that is experienced as life-giving,
numinous, miraculous.

In *Symbols of Transformation* (*CW,* Vol. 5, p. 432), Jung
suggests that sacrifice of consciousness is a necessary element
in psychological transformation:

> In the act of sacrifice, consciousness gives up its power and
> possession in the interest of the unconscious. This makes possi-
> ble a union of opposites resulting in a release of energy.

Jung characterizes the unconscious nature of transformation
when he says (ibid., p. 429),

> The essence and motive force of the sacrificial drama consist
> in an unconscious transformation of energy of which the ego
> becomes aware in much the same way as sailors are made aware
> of a volcanic upheaval under the sea.

His study of alchemy with its hermetically sealed vessel also
indicates the unconscious nature of transformation. The
themes of the fall of the dominant, of the death of the old king
and rebirth of the new, and others, suggest the necessity of
the sacrifice of a prevailing conscious attitude in the interest
of wholeness (*CW,* Vol. 12, pp. 327–356). In this case, the
symbolic "king," i.e., the dominant attitude that must be sacrificed, would be the conscious attitude that cognitive intellectual power alone can provide wholeness of personality; that
ego-consciousness without relation to the unconscious or
transpersonal can provide meaning.

The willingness of the patient to forgo interpretation of the
sand pictures, and to keep the inner alchemical process sealed
is just such a sacrifice.

The very act of playing is a submission of the autonomous
ego to the service of creative imagination, the freeing and

forming power of the Self. Playing requires an attitude or a condition of relatedness to the inner nonrational playful impulse and a willingness to give it concrete expression.

Sandplay also appears to provide a containing vessel that can transform boundless fantasy into focused and creative energy. The making of a picture is in itself a forming and creative act. The transposition of psychological complexes or conflicts from the inner, nonmaterial world to the concrete outer world seems to bring about a change in the dynamics of the unconscious. When an inner archetypal content takes an outer concrete form, it becomes symbolically objectified; this seems to cause a change in the inner dynamics, as if something moves and loosens the psychological logjam.

An instance of this phenomenon occurred with a patient who came into therapy with a long history of psychiatric care. There were frequent periods of anxiety, depression and disassociation that required antipsychotic medication, which kept him marginally functional.

He came to see me because he was depressed, extremely anxious and he felt himself sliding toward a psychotic episode. He was hoping he could avert it without medication. His psychiatrist was supportive and agreed that he might try. One day, shortly after we began seeing each other, he came in despair because he felt himself becoming nonfunctional, totally helpless.

Ordinarily, one does not use the sand tray for the first time under these circumstances because it can overstimulate the already overactive unconscious. However, I felt there was not much to lose and suggested he might like to try making his first sand picture. He said he was willing to try anything.

He stood staring at the tray for a while and then ran his hands into the sand. He caressed it, felt it, ran his hands through it as though discovering the texture of sand for the first time in his life. Just having his hands in it seemed to satisfy some hunger.

His pleasure was obvious as he kept finding new ways to experiment and feel the sand texture. Finally, he began pushing it and molding it in a very energetic way that astonished me, since just moments before he had been so listless.

He made the following picture:

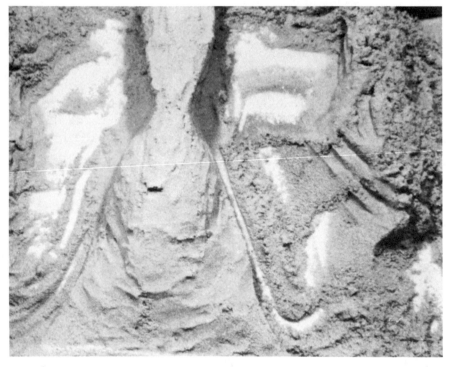

3. It's a female. It's a goddess.

After staring at it for a while, he finally said very quietly, "It's a female." Silence. Then, "It's a goddess, like I've seen in pictures of cave drawings. I wonder why I did that." Then, with some affect and a smile, he said, "My God, I made something! It pulled me out of myself! Maybe it's not so bad as I thought.''

This was a beginning. It was as though the unconscious had found a concrete representative and had, at least for now, lost its threatening aspect.

Jung offered an explanation of this phenomenon when he wrote of using painting as a way of distancing psychotic patients in relapse from the overwhelming power of the unconscious (*CW,* Vol. 3, p. 260, par. 562):

> In this way the apparently incomprehensible and unmanageable chaos of his total situation is visualized and objectified. . . . The effect of this method is evidently due to the fact that the originally chaotic or frightening impression is replaced by the picture, which, as it were, covers it up. The tremendum is spellbound by it, made harmless and familiar, and whenever the patient is reminded of this original experience by its menacing emotional effects, the picture he has made interposes itself between him and the experience and keeps his terror at bay.

9. A BRIDGE TO THE WORLD

The transposition of inner content into concrete outer form makes the inner content an outer reality and this outer reality, in turn, becomes a bridge or mediator to the world.

One patient actually depicted the bridge to what she called "the outside." This woman, in early thirties and unemployed, had been reclusive and tended toward a masculine identity. She was uncertain as to what being a woman meant to her and looked down on women. She wore pants exclusively and affected a tough-guy demeanor. She liked to play in the sand and over a two-year period created many pictures, making much progress during this time. She found a job in her field and after a courageous struggle with her fears, functioned quite well in it. Gradually she became aware and more accepting of her own feeling and femininity. In general, she seemed on the verge of stepping into the world in a new way.

One day she created an amphitheatre and stage in the sand and said, "It is the stage of life—where you play out all the characters in you." She spoke then of her longtime secret desire to be an actress.

4. The stage where you play out all the characters in you.

5. A bridge to cross.

The following week she formed an anchor-shaped bridge in the sand tray with a little girl on the bridge.

She told the following story about the picture:

Once there was a little girl who was not allowed to be a little girl. One part lived on one shore, and the other part lived on the other, and there was no way to get together. Then a bridge appeared in an anchor shape. It was a dark, misty night. The little girl went to look at the river. She had an overwhelming desire to cross the bridge because that's what bridges are for. It was a long, long bridge and she was wearing a ridiculous pink dress, but she went.

Shortly thereafter, the patient appeared for her session in the first dress she had worn in years. Within a few weeks, she joined an acting class with the idea of exploring her own emotions and relating to people in a structured setting "just to see what happens."

In providing a bridge to the world, the sand tray may serve as a "transitional object" as defined by the English child analyst, D. W. Winnicott. The transitional object is the first object that the infant perceives as "not-me," as not an extension of himself in contradistinction to his mother whom he does perceive as part of himself. In early childhood it is the soft cuddly animal, the teddy bear, that is separate, that can be embraced or abused and is *totally subject to the child's will.*

Winnicott (1975, p. 230) defines the transitional object as "an intermediate area of experiencing to which inner reality and external life both contribute. It is an area which is *not challenged, because no claim is made on its behalf except that it shall exist* as a resting place for the individual engaged in the perpetual human task of keeping inner and outer reality separate but related."

Winnicott suggests that the transitional object enables the child's development away from identification with the mother into an ego state capable of making the distinction between that which is I and not-I; which is, in turn, the basis for the

capacity to relate to, rather than identify with, inner contents
and outer reality and to discriminate between them.

As the child develops, the transitional object is decathected,
that is, the emotional energy invested in it is withdrawn into
the developing ego. The importance of the transitional object
dissipates because its meaning has been absorbed into the ego
and then diffused outward to the world. According to Winnicott, in effect, then, the transitional object leads the child
into the world (p. 230).

All of the above suggests that within the reconstituted mother-
child unity of sandplay therapy, the sand tray at a certain
point, when the ego is ready, may become a transitional object
leading out to the world as described above.

One of the features of the transitional object is that it accompanies the child in his separation from the mother and that at
some point it may even become more important than the
mother is, as the child exercises absolute and independent
power over it.

At least in some instances the sand tray acts as a transitional
object in that it replaces, to some extent, the person of the
therapist. One might even say the *transference* moves at least
partially from the person of the therapist to the sand tray as
it becomes an independent object. Not infrequently patients
report that they consciously carry an image of the sand tray
in their minds. They may focus on and reexperience some
part of a picture they have made, or change it, or they may
make imaginary new pictures which they often then create in
reality at the next opportunity.

Because of the nonrational, empathic nature of sandplay,
the transference can have a particularly intimate quality. Yet
less dependency seems to be engendered. One patient said,
"I woke up with an idea for a sand picture and I felt wonderful.
I felt I had created something all by myself."

Sometimes the transference seems to include both the person
of the therapist and the sand tray. Another patient who lived

a long distance away and could fly in for therapy just once a month said, "It's okay. I carry the tray in my head and play things out in it and I feel better."

10. A SAFE OUTLET FOR AGGRESSION

The free and protected space of sandplay provides a safe and sealed container where unredeemed demonic energies can be transformed by enabling the expression and playing out of repressed aggressive needs. It offers the possibility of acting out an inner impulse safely.

One highly repressed patient used a large knife to stab a large potato in the sand tray. The act discharged a powerful destructive impulse, after which there was a distinct elevation of mood, more direct verbal communication and a clearly stronger commitment to the therapeutic process.

Another male patient in his twenties had been in Jungian analysis for one year in another city. The patient had a very strong transference to his nurturing male analyst and felt very positively about his analytical experience. However, he had to leave that city and his analyst suggested that he continue his therapy with a woman when he moved. He came, resentful

6.   Discharging destructive impulses.

at having had to leave his previous therapy, extremely guarded and defensive with me because of a very powerful negative mother complex that he was unable to resolve. Caught in the matriarchal level of consciousness, he was unable to function professionally or socially. Having failed his professional licensing examination, he was very discouraged about trying again, nor could he find a job, so he was forced to live with his parents.

He lived largely as an emotional and social isolate, spending most of his days in fantasies in which he was either the saintly hero or the tortured victim.

He had a hard time being with me at the beginning of our work together because his severely negative mother complex was activated by the mere sight of me. However, he was fascinated by the sand tray and I hoped his pent-up rage and aggression might be played out there.

From the beginning I listened attentively to his dreams and fantasies. But I did not interpret them. I concentrated on our relationship and his interpersonal relationships in general. I also encouraged whatever concrete daily activity he could bring himself to do, i.e., job-seeking efforts, seeing a friend, etc.

In his first sand picture, at his second session, a crusader on his way to Jerusalem decapitated a beautiful blonde princess.

7. Decapitation—the beginning of a process.
   A crusader on his way to Jerusalem.

Almost incapacitated by his ambivalence, repulsion and attraction to the feminine in general and his mother in particular, this symbolic acting out of victory over the threat seemed to release him.

Thereafter, he seemed free to vent his aggression toward me overtly. He spent many of his hours excoriating me for not being his old analyst, for not confronting him, for confronting him too much, for not being "smart" enough, for being too intellectual, for either talking too much or not enough.

During this cathartic period, his fantasies changed character and a new recurring figure appeared; a young Indian man who left his family and discovered his own protective cave where he could freely come and go.

In his second picture, a few weeks later, he depicted the young man and an older wise man about to enter a walled central forest.

The story relating to the picture was that the old man taught him how "to be a tree"; that he must learn to accept and live the cyclical vicissitudes of life. At this point he decided to take the state professional exam again and shortly thereafter found a part-time job in his profession.

He subsequently passed the exam and the part-time job eventually developed into a responsible position. At this time he had a fantasy in which an eagle came to the young Indian man. The young man made a relationship with the great bird, and the eagle became his special protector.

Some 10 months after coming into therapy, he moved into his own apartment. He wished to interrupt his therapy for a while so that he could afford to furnish his apartment. In addition, he wanted to see how well he could manage on his own. We agreed that he would check in from time to time, which he has done.

Shortly after interrupting his therapy, he sent me a gift for my collection, a figure of a naked tiny baby. A few months later when he came to check in, he reported that his job was going quite well and that he had begun an important relation-

8. How to be a tree.

ship with a woman. He made his third picture. He placed the figure of the infant that he had sent me in the center of an otherwise empty sand tray.

This young man came from an affluent family where no one ever expressed unpleasant feelings, certainly nothing aggressive. He felt unable to meet the male standard set by his father, who was very successful. Hence, the patient was emotionally tied to a mother who controlled him via the "sensitivity of her feelings."

To express anger or aggression toward her was unthinkable. Consciously he both loved and abhorred her. At the same time he had introjected from her an unrealistic ideal of romantic femininity that ill-fitted him for dealing with his own feminine component or women in the world.

The patient, caught in the uroboric-matriarchal state, was indeed threatened by the feminine. I believe the safety of the sand tray enabled the playing out of powerful aggression that needed some safe outlet.

After the beheading of the beautiful blonde princess, which represented his own ideal and romanticized head-image of the feminine, he felt strong enough to vent his suppressed aggression to a concrete woman who happened to be his therapist.

This safe acting-out of confrontation with the feminine made possible the move out of the uroboric-matriarchal stage to the beginning of the patriarchal stage, represented by the wise old man's teaching on how to become a tree, and the eagle protecting the young Indian. This enabled the subsequent birth of the male ego, symbolized by the picture of the naked infant. It was no accident that shortly thereafter he brought me as a gift a picture postcard of Perseus holding the head of Medusa. Perseus overcame the threatening terrible aspect of the feminine by using his shield as a mirror to see what he was doing as he cut off her head (since it was death to look directly at Medusa). It occurred to me that perhaps the sand tray had been the patient's mirror.

9.

9 a.

Rebirth of ego.

11. FEELING, CREATING, CENTERING

In sandplay, the adult plays as does a child, with seriousness. The playing aspect seems to provide access or an initiatory rite of entry for adults into feeling, affect and the world of childhood. Lost memories are found again, repressed fantasies are released and possibilities of reconciliation occur. Paradoxically, sandplay seems to enhance the capacity to distinguish between illusion and reality.

THE RECOVERY OF FEELING

One insecure underachieving young woman in her late twenties sought her sense of identity and security from men. Her father had died when she was a young child and her mother had been remarried twice to men who had not provided any paternal parenting.

The patient, while being extremely critical of her mother, unconsciously identified with her mother's materialistic values.

Like her mother, she used men to provide security and self-esteem—a woman without a man was a loser, an object of pity and condescension. Men were not to be trusted. One must always control them because the interesting ones "let you down or abandoned you."

Highly defended and extremely needy emotionally, she was currently involved in a destructive relationship and unable to extricate herself. Fearful of abandonment and unable to trust men, she was victimized by her passions. Very intelligent, she had come to the conclusion, "It all has something to do with my father dying when I was so young." She was, however, unable to feel anything about her father and, in fact, remembered little about him.

Her first sand picture consisted of a house with a father figure, two little girls, and a mother.

She identified the little girl next to the father as herself. Contemplation of the picture seemed to dissolve her memory

10. The family.

block and her frozen feelings. She remembered incident after incident with her father and, in fact, recalled that she had been his favorite. There were tears.

10a. Father and daughter.

Her second picture, made the following week, consisted of a frightened little girl alone in the woods.

11.   Alone in the woods.

11a. Detail.

There were more tears and an acknowledgment of her own inner fear and loneliness. She was now able to recognize that her mother had also been lost and frightened when her father died, and the patient was able to forgive her for her inadequacies. The patient was able to recognize that the needy child still existed within her self and to take responsibility for its psychological care and feeding.

Thereafter she was able to give up the illusory security of the unsatisfactory relationship and to go on alone with the new attitude of self-sufficiency as illustrated in her third and last picture, in which she included a positive male figure.

12. A new attitude.

THE ACT OF CREATING

The act of doing, in itself, seems to foster a growing sense of creativity which, in turn, reinforces the ego and improves the patient's self-image and self-confidence. A good deal of satisfaction and release of tension seems to evolve out of the mere act of creation.

The doing aspect of sandplay seems particularly effective in cases where the patient feels helpless in the face of reality (see Chapter 8). It is also effective in coagulating or bringing into awareness a state of development that has been readying itself:

A woman in her early forties, highly *extraverted* and very gifted, fled responsibility for her own gifts and lived through and for others, particularly her husband. With no authentic sense of herself, she borrowed security and authority from her husband's achievements, status and prestige.

He had lost respect for her and the marriage was threatened. After three months of therapy she had begun to take some steps toward a more independent stance, and the relationship had improved. But she still looked back on the early years of the marriage as idyllic.

At this point she made a sand picture of a small town with no people in it and with a well near the center.

At first she said it reminded her of a small town where she and her husband had been in the "good time." Then she looked at the picture again and said, "No, this is my own town where there are no people. Here I can do what I wish." There was a long silence. Then she said, "The good time is now."

13.   The good time is now.

A FORM OF MEDITATION

Sandplay seems to serve a meditative purpose similar to that of a mandala. It fosters sensitivity to inner images, a condition of relatedness to the inner world. Its concreteness seems to encourage a state of absorption and relaxed concentration; of non-rational awareness. One stands before the empty sand tray or the full shelves of figures and waits for an idea or an image. Or one awakens in the morning with an idea or an image to be concretized in the sand tray. When one completes a picture one feels a release of tension. And at that moment one realizes that the picture represents at least some aspect of one's inner being. One is made aware, therefore, of that inner condition, feeling, mood, etc.

The sand tray acts as a focus of attention that encourages centering. Its physical boundaries, around an enclosed space, keep out distractions. As such, it has a distinctly quieting and focusing effect that seems to facilitate penetration into the transpersonal level of the psyche.

REDIRECTING ENERGY

If a *union of opposites* releases energy, as Jung has said (*CW*, Vol. 5, par. 671), then sandplay would seem to offer several energy-releasing possibilities since, by its very nature, it mediates between opposites.: horizontal and vertical dimensions, the visible and the invisible, mystery and concrete reality, inner impulse and outer reality, mind and body (idea and physical expression), consciousness and the unconscious.

Sandplay in itself seems to offer a metaphorical union of the masculine and feminine in that it combines mind/spirit and body, masculine and feminine elements: the feminine material earth is acted upon by the non-material masculine mind; the masculine idea or abstraction is given concrete feminine expression; consciousness and the unconscious meet concretely.

Perhaps the most telling union of opposites lies in the *synchronistic* elements of sandplay. Kalff has said (conversation,

June 1972):

Sandplay is a *synchronistic event* in that there is a simultaneous psychophysical phenomenon. The inner image is given physical expression. With each synchronistic event, the next step is born. The synthesis between the psychic and the physical becomes the thesis for the next step in the process.

There is a healing synchronistic moment when the inner and outer happen simultaneously; that is, the patient reveals the inner subjective state at the same moment that the therapist outside understands it. The synchronous event, in completing a gestalt, in itself, makes possible and provides momentum toward the next developmental step.

Neumann (*The Child,* p. 146) suggests that the evolving ego's relation to the world and to the unconscious undergoes continuous transformation based on archetypal patterns and that these transformations occur unconsciously and automatically given the proper activating circumstances.

If neuroses can be seen as energy misdirected or misused, if transformation includes a redirecting of energy into creative channels and unconscious development of the personality, sandplay offers at least some of the elements that enable transformation.

12. RESISTANCE

Some inarticulate patients turn to the sand tray with relief since self-expression through language is so fraught with anxiety for them. Visually creative people also welcome sandplay and are quickly absorbed in it. For the majority, however, who as products of an intellectual/technological age have been conditioned away from instinctual, nonverbal modes of experience, who have little or no relationship with their imaginations, and have forgotten how to play, courage is required to face the emptiness of the sand tray, that is, to be thrown back on their own creative resources. Patients sense that this process will have more meaning for them personally than seems to be the case.

Therefore, as in all forms of therapy, it is important to establish a trusting relationship as quickly as possible. The quick formation of a therapeutic alliance is particularly important for success-oriented, intellectual and verbal personalities, since noninterpretation can be particularly anxiety-provoking. For them, childlike playing is a "waste of time." On the other hand, they sense that the concrete products of "just playing" may be revealing in a way that they cannot control. One patient, a writer, said recently, "This thing is so scary because you know it's going to reveal more than words can."

Intellectuals are accustomed to controlling with words. Nonrational, nonverbal experience for them represents a loss of command not easily borne.

The loss of control when there are no words is emphasized by Paolo Aite in an article in the *Journal of Analytical Psychology* (October 1978, p. 35), where he points out that "communication mediated by the imagination overcomes defenses in patients' talk; defenses which often also influence how the patient recounts dreams."

Aite also says that in his experience patients use sandplay as a form of resistance when they make pictures to meet the real or supposed expectations of the analyst. I find that this happens particularly when patients have knowledge of symbols. However, more often than not, the pictures do not turn out as planned. Even when they do, such pictures with a plethora of "Jungian" symbolism are recognizable. Usually, after a few such attempts, the patients begin to make pictures that genuinely reflect something of their inner states because they discover a pleasurable release of tension when a feeling or impulse has been truly expressed.

Generally, I have found that when patients do try to use sandplay as a diversionary tactic, the pictures give some hint of the problem anyway.

Strong and consistent conscious resistance to doing sandplay should be respected. Loss of verbal control may simply be too threatening for some patients; others may be so vulnerable to "flooding" by the unconscious that they feel immediately threatened by any limitation of ego control. This would apply to severely borderline patients or those on a prepsychotic state.

In other cases, although sandplay does open the world of fantasy, in my experience there does not appear to be much danger of the patient being overwhelmed by the unconscious.

Schizophrenics exhibit marked resistance to sandplay. They often speak at great length before starting. There is often a pronounced lack of absorption in the play itself.

When they finally make the pictures, they generally ignore the sand, using it as they would any other surface. They build *on* the sand rather than *in* it. They often prefer the sand to be dry. They generally avoid touching the sand, which points to a symbolic disconnection with the earth and reality.

Their pictures as a rule lack margins. Often everything is crowded to the very edge. The borders are filled, as though the patients are fearful of something penetrating. Usually, no central figures appear, nor is there a centering in the arrangement of the pictures.

The characteristics described above may appear in pictures of nonschizophrenics in a "flooded" state. However, Kalff has pointed out that a characteristic feature of the schizophrenic patient is that a whole process may appear to take place in the sand tray, but there is no perceptible change in the personality. The phenomenon suggests that the unconscious, due to its autonomy, is responsive, but that the ego in such cases is unable to integrate the experience.

Sandplay is not effective with all patients, nor is any other psychotherapeutic mode, but when the process does take hold, it seems to operate in the V-shaped manner described by Kalff, that is, the process moves down into the depths of the personality to the transpersonal and then upward and out again toward engagement with the here and now, with life as it is.

13. A COMPARISON OF VERBAL ANALYSIS AND SANDPLAY

In sandplay, one starts at a given point and works down through the complexes and repression to reach the source, the union of opposites, the totality which is innate and a priori. Then one moves up again on the vegetative level in a preconscious way.—Kalff (conversation, June 1972).

DEVELOPMENTAL STAGES

As in a verbal analysis, the stages in the sandplay process do not appear as discrete entities nor in a strictly given order. A recurring general outline can be discerned which is rather like a spiral in that the same structural elements of the personality appear in symbolic form at different levels of development. However, there are differences between the stages of a classical verbal analysis and sandplay therapy, and they will be described in this chapter.

Through dream interpretation and the analytical dialogue, the patient in verbal analysis is more or less conscious of his development as it occurs. Sandplay therapy is largely experienced by the patient subliminally (vegetatively). Only later in the process is there more consciousness and ego-activity on the part of the patient.

As in verbal analysis, not all sandplay patients go through all the stages or complete a sandplay process. Some do sandplay only at times of crisis. Some patients have limited goals or limited time; they come with a particular problem to solve and they work until it is solved and then terminate therapy. Some never really engage with sandplay. Some have a limited developmental potential.

It must be emphasized that the stages described here merge and overlap so that one picture more often than not shows representations of several stages or elements in various evolutionary states.

The first pictures in the sandplay process are usually realistic scenes and, as in initial dreams, may give indications of the problems and their possible resolution.

The pictures in the second phase often indicate rapid penetration into deeper levels of the personality, into the *shadow* (personal unconscious). The pictures may have a chaotic quality now as though the patient had entered his own underworld and touched untapped raw energies. As the process moves on, one also begins to see varying degrees of resolution of problems and complexes.

This, in turn, seems to release more energy which enables a still deeper descent into the psyche to the extent that the Self or totality can be constellated and touched.

This stage, at the deepest level, may be represented in the sand tray in numerous ways, but usually appears in images of centering or unions of opposites, or overtly religious symbols such as Christ, Buddha, mandalas, etc. A numinous experience occurs together with the awakening of a religious impulse. The patient has a sense of having touched "home," of having been guided by a suprapersonal power, and a paradoxical change occurs. The patient's consciousness (ego), having experienced the greater Self, gives up its autonomy, and paradoxically, at the same moment, experiences itself as stronger because of a feeling of being supported by that same transpersonal power to which it has surrendered. The person gains, then, a new sense of order and security and a new sense of his own worth. It is this phenomenon that Kalff has called "the relativization of the ego." It is as though a coagulation occurs, in which the ego finds its right size and function. The ego no longer envisions itself as the supreme power within the personality, but as evolving out of the unconscious and in daily relation to it.

The above-described experience is very similar to the Self-experience that occurs in a verbal analysis, with some differences: In sandplay, it often occurs more quickly. Also, the therapist sometimes can see it approaching as centering and organization begin to appear in the pictures after the chaotic stage subsides. (The actual manifestation of the Self, however much hinted at and anticipated, remains a moving experience for both patient and therapist.)

The particular virtue of the Self-constellation in sandplay, however, lies in its concrete visibility. This becomes especially clear when the slides are being shown. The experience of the transpersonal is then reiterated and reinforced in a conscious way. Once again, the patient recognizes and experiences the "otherness" of what has happened when he now consciously retraces his past. He literally sees what has taken place within him and realizes that it happened autonomously since there was no interpretation and all happened unconsciously.

There is almost invariably a sense of awe and surprise at the richness within him. A new relationship with his own imagination and inner being is born, and he gains a new sense of his worth and strength because he literally sees it. Based on his own experience, he begins to sense that there really is a healing and organizing factor within that transcends his ego-consciousness and that it can be trusted; that perhaps even life can be trusted; that there may be hidden meaning in even unfortunate or trivial events; that much of what happens to him is not necessarily determined by consciousness alone. This concrete evidence of the numinous and the experience with it, is a major event in relatedness to the unconscious and the Self, which is the core of both sandplay therapy and the Jungian analytical process.

After the constellation of the Self, one can usually see the emergence of the reborn ego in the sand pictures. Sometimes, although not always, the patient chooses a single figure of the same gender with which he or she now consciously identifies, and which appears regularly in the ongoing process.

Subsequent pictures take on a more creative character. They are better organized and the patient relates to them differently. The sandplay process becomes progressive in that the ego takes a more active stance in relation to both the inner and outer worlds.

At the beginning stages of sandplay, the patient's engagement has a passive quality. In playing out his fantasy, he *projects* onto the figures. With the emergence of the "new" ego, the patient has more energy, awareness, and assurance. He consciously recognizes that he is involved in a meaningful process, that the pictures represent himself, that the figures are metaphors for aspects of himself and that he can interact with them and use them to express himself.[1]

After the emergence of the ego, figures or symbols of the opposite sex begin to appear regularly and in orderly fashion,

---

[1]Michael Fordham (1956, pp. 207–208) distinguishes between what he calls imaginative activity and active imagination. In imaginative activity, a passive ego plays out a fantasy. In active imagination there is an active ego-engagement and interaction with the fantasy. It may be that in the early stage of the sandplay process imaginative activity occurs and that active imagination begins only after the constellation of the Self and the emergence of the new ego.

indicating the differentiation of the masculine-feminine, contra-sexual animus/anima factors.

Sometimes differentiation of shadow and contrasexual components begins on the very primitive vegetative level with primal kinds of animals. These contents evolve into higher animal levels and then into human figures. As the contrasexual, animus/anima factors develop, patients become more aware of creative stirrings and actively begin to seek constructive outlets in life for their newly generated energy. New attitudes and feelings are engendered and the patient begins to take a more active role in life. As the process draws to a close, spiritual figures or abstract religious symbols may reappear, or appear for the first time.

A peculiar feature of the sandplay process is that contrasexual differentiation occurs after or at about the same time as the manifestation of the Self and the emergence of the new ego. This differs from verbal analysis wherein the differentiation of the contrasexual animus/anima usually precedes the constellation of the Self and is the gateway to it.

This "peculiarity" would seem to support the thesis that sandplay therapy operates at a profound level; that it does indeed reconstitute the mother-child unity, enabling (1) the constellation of the Self, (2) the emergence of a new ego and (3) the differentiation of the contrasexual elements.

It strikes me that this developmental sequence was indicated by Neumann in *The Child* as the natural development of normal children. In this case the constellation of the Self and the emergence of a sound ego act as the foundation from which the incarnated contrasexual elements can be differentiated, so that the creative aspects of the animus/anima can be activated to enrich ego-consciousness rather than dominate it, as it does when the ego is weak.

There are other constructs of Neumann that appear to be illustrated by sandplay therapy. In *The Origins and History of Consciousness* (p. 286), he defines the self-organizing capacity of the psyche as the process of centroversion: "the innate tendency of a whole to create unity within its parts and to synthesize their differences into unified systems." This biologically determined dynamism expresses itself in the psyche as the drive toward wholeness (p. 405).

He goes on to say (p. 287) that "the specific trend of centroversion asserts itself *only* during a *formative* stage, at which time a visible center appears. . . ." In fact, it is "centroversion which sets ego development in motion within the psyche and thrusts the ego complex and consciousness into the foreground" (*The Child*, p. 139).

One can literally see this process of centroversion or organization-out-of-chaos occur in almost every series of pictures where the process has taken hold.

In *The Child* (p. 136), Neumann suggests that the emergence of the ego reflects the development of the personality from the uroboric-matriarchal to the patriarchal level of the psyche. Here sandplay seems to corroborate Neumann's constructs again. The appearance of earth-water vegetative symbols, followed by the appearance of patriarchal sky-sun symbolism, indicates movement out of the matriarchate. The appearance of patriarchal symbolism in the pictures of both men and women seems to mark the emergence of a relatively independent ego. As the ego develops further, masculine and feminine symbols appear in the same picture in relation to each other, indicating a more balanced and dynamic interaction between these characteristics, a union of opposites, within the personality.

When this point is attained, slides of the sand pictures can be shown and explanations and interpretations given. The assumption here is that an ego now exists that is capable of integrating heretofore unconscious material.

AN UNGUIDED WAY TO SELF

Living as we do in an extraverted, materialistic, media-dominated society, the capacity for inner experience is conditioned out of us at an early age. Even under the best of circumstances we are trained from the beginning to look for and listen to outer guidance. We are accustomed to listening to what others say.

Sandplay provides a safe, externally *unguided* way to our own depths. Interpretations delayed until after constellation of the Self has occurred can be heard and imprinted in a different way because an inner sense of security has developed. Then the ego is ready to integrate information, to be responsible for what it knows. Knowledge and insight become usable rather than wearable. We have all met analysands who "talk" a good analysis, who "understand" themselves and their complexes, but whose behavior and state of relatedness to themselves and others tends to give psychoanalysis, and psychotherapy in general, a bad name. When the Self is operational and supportive, there is less chance of identifying with what one is told or being unduly influenced by the therapist. By the same token, there is less need for defensive rejection of new insights.

If at a certain point in the process, the sand tray serves as a transitional object, it fosters independence at the same time that it offers security.

One other advantage of sandplay may be that there are fewer words, for words may stand in the way of immediate communication. A verbal description of an image is, at best, a step removed. Words are a name or concept of something, not the thing itself. Words may bring semantic difficulties that interfere with communication. A concrete representation of a visual image carries an immediacy of shared experience between patient and therapist that words may dilute. The language of the unconscious, after all, is the image.

The speed and depth at which sandplay operates in *some* (not all) patients is startling. One can only conjecture as to why . . .

Perhaps the concentration of attention and the activation of the imaginative creative faculties within the free and protected space generates or frees enough *libido* (psychic energy) to loosen the grip of the complexes relatively quickly, as though the healing process were activated through exercise of the imagination.

Perhaps, as suggested earlier, the concrete enactment in sensate reality in sandplay does stimulate archetypal activity which may manifest in dreams or directly into behavior, for in some cases sandplay provides the cutting edge of the therapeutic process; that is, themes appear in sand pictures before they appear in dreams.

In any event, at least in some cases, the interaction between sandplay and verbal analysis appears to have a synergistic effect.

A FEW WORDS OF CAUTION

Sandplay operates at a primitive level of the psyche. Therefore, the stages of development as described here should be seen as developments in potentia only. What they represent in each individual needs to be carefully integrated into consciousness and into everyday life. Responsibility must be taken for these contents and that takes effort and time.

As centering begins and the constellation of the Self approaches, a considerable amount of physical and psychological energy is released. There is a feeling of well-being, of rebirth. I think at that moment, birth is the operative word. One is psychologically about two years old, full of energy and prepared to pour it into almost any likely or unlikely project.

I mistakenly poured the energy into the renovation of a big old house in the country that turned out to be a painful comedy of errors. It happened because I had to leave Zurich (the first time) before the process was finished.

On the other hand, one patient of mine, an artist, completely altered her method of working, a change that took several hard years to complete.

The patient whose case is presented in Part II of this book started to write poetry quite spontaneously and ultimately changed his domicile and the direction of his work. This is not to imply that these rather dramatic events happen in all cases, but they can and do.

It is important that a focus be found for this energy—some creative and meaningful outlet. If an independent creative channel does not suggest itself spontaneously, then perhaps the therapist can suggest something of a structured nature: classes in the learning of a craft or new skills, dance, or perhaps some kind of body work. Patients' bodies often come alive, and it is helpful for them to experience them in new and vital ways. If the therapist does not recognize the energic phenomenon, if no appropriate outlet is found, there is a real danger of *inflation* or misuse of the energy, with potentially serious consequences. This is particularly so since so much of the process happens unconsciously.

The psychological state at this time in the process is difficult to describe or communicate. That is just one reason why the therapist himself should have experienced the sandplay therapy process.

14. OVERVIEW

Precisely because they evolve out of a nonverbal, nonrational autonomous process with little possibility of undue influence on the part of the therapist, the stages of development, as they appear in sandplay therapy, lend credence to Neumann's theories regarding the critical importance of the mother-child unity, the constellation of the Self as the prerequisite of the emergence of the true ego, and the development of the ego from the uroboric-matriarchal to the patriarchal levels of the psyche. Sandplay also offers corroborative evidence that early development of the personality is an essentially unconscious, archetypally determined process.

The appearance of a centering phenomenon in the sand pictures supports Neumann's theory of centroversion, which was, in turn, based on Jung's postulate of an innate ordering process within the human personality.

Sand pictures created in the autonomous externally unguided sandplay process indicate penetration into a transpersonal level of the personality, with a concomitant numinous experience by the patient (not unlike that described by those who feel they have received divine grace). This phenomenon presents tangible evidence of the validity of Jung's assertion of an innate religious impulse in the human psyche.

Sandplay therapy is an efficient modality that provides:

- Direct access to the personal inner world of impulse and feeling. It provides access to the creative playworld of childhood as well as reasonably safe entry into the deeper archetypal realm, since it concretizes and delimits the archetypal language of images. It also acts as a mediator or bridge to the outer world.

- An instrumentality for the recovery of the specifically feminine dimension of the psyche.

- A means of repairing damage to the mother-image that would otherwise impair fulfillment of the potentiality of the whole personality. It does this by reconstituting the mother-child unity that enables the constellation of the Self which is the forerunner of the development of a healthy ego.

- Activation of a natural, self-healing capacity of the psyche.

- A means of reaching and experiencing the transpersonal realm of the psyche. This produces "relativization of the ego" and a more naturally balanced relationship between the ego and the Self.

- An opportunity for inarticulate patients to emerge from inner isolation through the unspoken communication made possible via sand pictures. It is especially helpful when the intuitive or empathic capacities of the analyst are not highly developed, since sand pictures offer *concrete* expression of the patient's situation.

- A rechanneling and/or transformation of blocked energy.

- A means of self-discovery and awakening of creative capacities with minimal influence by the therapist: A rite of passage such as Jung himself described in *Memories, Dreams, Reflections* when painting a picture or carving in stone: "each such experience proved to be a rite d'entree for the ideas and works that followed hard upon it."

- At the very least, opportunity for creative nonrational experience as a counterweight to collective overemphasis on the ego-oriented intellect.

Sandplay therapy accelerates the individuation process since it appears to bypass—at least to some extent—resolution of complexes, integration of the shadow, and the differentiation of the negative and positive aspects of the animus/anima. It seems to move in a more direct line toward the constellation of the Self and the renewal of the ego.

Sandplay therapy is essentially an unconscious, or at some stages, a semiconscious process. It has an almost magical attraction for children and a powerful efficacy. In childhood, the ego is naturally still largely contained in the unconscious out of which it slowly evolves. In children, the preponderance of the unconscious and the slow emergence of the ego is a normal, natural, autonomous development. For children, therefore, healing and the constellation and positive activation of the Self appears to provide a sound basis out of which a healthy ego and mature consciousness will emerge naturally.

With some adults sandplay therapy, in a relatively short time, enables a person to go on with his life with a new trust in his own potentialities and a new sense of inner support. In these circumstances, it would be well to remember the necessity of finding a creative gradient or outlet for the energy released in the sandplay process. Otherwise, it may be dissipated in meaningless activity. It may be appropriated by an unresolved complex or by the ego which then becomes unrealistically inflated.

I have noticed a phenomenon in my practice that seems to support the idea of sandplay as a healing modality. I have found that some adult patients who engage in sandplay successfully tend to lose intensity of interest in making sand pictures soon after a constellation of the Self and the emergence of a more stable ego. Except for moments of great emotional intensity or periods of transition, when they turn back to the sand trays, they become much more interested in analyzing their dreams, expanding and strengthening ego-consciousness and cognitive understanding, and in making concrete choices and decisions in their everyday lives. The process now moves progressively towards concrete reality and everyday life as the patient strives to integrate his therapeutic experience into his life. It is as though the wounded child within has been healed and the patient now wishes to take up adult life in a more conscious way. It appears that the individuation process had begun via sandplay on the nonverbal, matriarchal level and that it now wants to continue in the more cerebral and sensate way that is characteristic of the patriarchal level of consciousness hypothesized by Neumann—one more corroboration of his concepts.

Sandplay heals wounds that have blocked normal development. It enables the constellation and positive activation of the Self and the emergence of a stable ego capable of relating equally to the outer material and inner spiritual worlds—to life in the here and now, and to the transpersonal dimension. At its best, sandplay therapy is a prime facilitator of the individuation process. At its least, it is an invaluable adjunctive modality.

PART II

CASE PRESENTATION

This case involved a relatively short process, consisting of 48 sessions over an 18-month period interrupted by a 5-month hiatus. It was chosen because it consists of a manageable number of pictures and because it illustrates some of the stages referred to in this paper. The stages were culled from clinical practice with a large number of patients. They do not always appear as described, nor are the pictures always as clearly demonstrative. This patient came with a capacity for symbolic realization and an active spiritual need. He had, too, a rich fantasy life that needed a container and focus so that it could become creative rather than threatening to him.

Interpretations, other than those I have presented of this case material and its symbols, certainly were, and are, possible. Other possibilities have not been included here because a comprehensive study of the symbolic meanings in this case was not the intent. This is as complete a record of the case as seemed feasible within the parameters of this book, the purpose of which has been to describe the practice of sandplay therapy as I practice it, within the context of Jungian analysis, to formulate certain of its basic concepts, and to offer some illustrative case material.

The patient was a young man in his twenties who consciously identified with his personal father and with the patriarchal archetype of the spirit. His was a problem of misdirected spirituality that was hampering his life and which required the recovery of the feminine in order to find some grounding in reality. It was as though the patient required a maternal container in order to separate from the father. The case involved the descent into the matriarchal level of the unconscious, followed by the reemergence or rebirth of the ego into a more solidly based patriarchal level of consciousness that included the reclaimed feminine, which in turn enabled a new supportive spirituality.

DESCRIPTION

The patient was 28 years old, unmarried and a professionally trained business man of pleasant appearance and demeanor. Although he lived in the city and worked in a sophisticated corporate office, he appeared for his mid-week analytical session wearing overalls and went to work in them.

PRESENTING PROBLEMS

At first he denied having any problems. He came because he felt he should know himself better in order to achieve his goal, which was to attain peace (nirvana) with his intellect. He denigrated his feelings and said he deliberately suppressed them because he thought feeling "messed up the clarity of life." He did admit to having some difficulty in a year-old ongoing relationship with a young woman who was pressing for marriage. Although he felt committed to her, he was suspicious of all social institutions that tended to restrict autonomy, and he was particularly wary of marriage. He did express some concern about "not being able to meet her emotional needs."

BACKGROUND AND RELEVANT DATA

The patient came from an upper middle-class, emotionally constricted Protestant family that was dominated by a rigid, patriarchal perfectionist father who was addressed as Sir. Sunday church attendance was mandatory. The father's *professed ideal was the control of all emotions by the mind.* He had achieved considerable professional and financial success and assumed his four sons would do the same.

Acceptance or approval in the family were contingent on the performance of family roles and functions *as designated by the father.* The mother, a dedicated *hausfrau,* both rigid and highly emotional, was an object of condescension by the domineering father, and had turned to an older son for comfort by the time the patient was born.

Early in life, the patient had assumed the role of the "good son" of the father and consciously identified with the father's values. The father's oft-repeated phrase was: " 'The Smiths' don't do things the way others do them. More is expected of us." The patient, cut off from his mother and the feminine (because she had turned to the older brother), was burdened not only with his father's extremely one-sided values, but also an obligation to fulfill a superior destiny, a sense of spiritual noblesse-oblige that reinforced his early identification with the spirit.

While excelling in academics and sports as a youth, the patient described himself as "somewhat of a loner" and a "late bloomer" sexually. He did not date at all until well into college and described himself as having had "a hard time of it socially."

At present, he was living with his girlfriend, and this was his first important involvement. Unaccustomed to experiencing and/or expressing feelings, he gave her authority over all matters pertaining to feeling or relationship. He tried to meet her emotional needs, but when he couldn't, he reacted with passive-resistant behavior that was typical for him: He would withdraw into silence or go out walking for hours, or he would avoid confrontation with her by engaging in obsessive-compulsive behavior; for instance, repetitious performance of household chores.

There were also many long, overwrought "intellectual" discussions between them regarding the nature of love and relationship. These became power struggles and merely aggravated their difficulties. After some weeks in therapy, the patient admitted that he was having difficulty with his job. He had been graduated from professional school with honors and held a prestigious position. However, he was habituated to marijuana, regularly smoking several times a day during working hours. He tended to spend much of his working day fantasizing, and then overcompensated for this by obsessive attention to details. He was unable to finish assignments satisfactorily and on time and was finding it increasingly difficult to maintain even a minimal level of productivity.

At the same time that he was undermining his present position and prejudicing his future in his profession, he had frequent fantasies in which he accomplished dangerous heroic feats. There were frequent dreams of levitating or of heroically flying bodily off cliffs. A case in point was a dream he had of running hand-in-hand with his girlfriend on a high plateau and then taking off into the air with her at the edge of a cliff: indicating that he was in danger of losing touch with reality.

He articulated grandiose ideas about life, wisdom and peace that were attempts to rationalize his behavior. For instance, "detachment" was an important idea to him and was used as a rationale for avoiding conformity or commitment. Any circumstance or social convention perceived as limiting his autonomy—e.g., holding a job and being answerable to a supervisor, wearing conventional clothes, or getting married—was met with *automatic* passive-aggressive resistance.

ASSESSMENT

The patient was highly defended and insisted for some weeks that he had come to discuss philosophical issues only. He would report dreams, but he wished to discuss *his interpretations of them.* Any suggestion that the dreams indicated that all might not be as he envisioned met with firm resistance. He was not prepared to acknowledge or deal with his shadow in any way. Biographical data were difficult to obtain because he felt it would be disloyal to discuss his family. In fact, he began to speak freely about his life and family only after he began to do sand pictures.

He was willing, however, to discuss his problems with his girlfriend in a guarded manner, and even finally to admit that a factor in his coming to therapy was the girl's insistence that he was "not meeting her needs." He did not consider that he had any unmet needs of his own since his goal of nirvana, "peace," required detachment, which meant self-sufficiency and not needing anything from anyone.

He presented a diagnostic picture of a severe inflation compensating for a pervasive underlying anxiety. He was using an obsessive-compulsive adjustment that was in danger of being overwhelmed by an active paranoid tendency. His intrusive fantasy life, the marijuana habituation, his grandiose intellectualizations which were almost word salads, his difficulty with feeling, with any form of authority or limitation of autonomy, all suggested a possible paranoid process that originated in the disassociation from his feelings and his need to rationalize his lack of emotional life and his inner isolation. In functional terms, he was woefully lacking in feeling and a sense of reality.

He seemed to me to be a classical victim of what Murray Stein, in *Fathers and Mothers* (pp.64–74), has called the Kronus aspect of "the devouring father." Kronus, in order to free himself, castrated his father and then he himself became the devouring father, eating his sons.

Stein suggests that the strategy of latter-day Kronuses with their sons is "to incorporate them and then to spiritualize or psychologize them thereby severing them from their instinctual origins" (p. 71). This patient, spiritually and psychologically devoured by his father, was as emotionally isolated and incapable of relating as Jonah was in the belly of the whale.

It is interesting that the patient's father was almost literally a Kronus figure in that he "psychologically" killed his own father. No mention was ever made of the paternal grandfather or of the father's family in general, nor were there any questions about the subject entertained in the household. The father's background remained a mystery as if he had sprung from the earth full-blown with no parents.

Little or no progress was made in the first few sessions because the patient dominated them with his mind in the same way his father dominated his household. Then the patient made his first sand picture.

The relatively few sand pictures (14), in this case, illustrate the stages of development in sandplay therapy.

1. An initial realistic scene hinting at problems and possible resolutions.
2. Descent into the personal unconscious (shadow), revealing problems and healing potentialities more clearly.
3. Partial resolution of a major complex.
4. Differentiation of the opposites, centering, constellation of the Self.
5. Emergence of the nascent ego and an ensuing struggle to differentiate masculine and feminine aspects of the personality.
6. Emergence of the anima/animus.
7. Relativization of the ego with respect to the transpersonal.
8. Emergence from the matriarchal toward the patriarchal level of consciousness.

PICTURE 1

Description

This is a scene of American Indians. On the right toward the center is an American Indian chief extending a peace pipe. Behind him is a tepee, and two women with a baby. The upper right quadrant contains an oak tree. Under the oak tree, in deep shadow, not easily discernible in this picture, sits an Indian brave alone, under the tree. Behind the tree are a male and female deer. The lower right quadrant contains an evergreen tree and behind it a horse, also not easily discernible in this picture. In the upper middle of the picture near the boundary of the box is a golden figure of Buddha. The upper left

1. An American Indian Scene

quadrant contains two nomadic Indian women leading horses that are drawing their supplies and belongings. They are approaching the Indian camp. In the lower part of the picture, toward the center, is a canoe with two white trappers. In the lower left quadrant is a very large tree. To the left of that is a barren tree, and hidden behind the two trees is a buffalo. It is obscured from the view of all the other figures in the picture.

Patient's Comments

The patient said that this was a peaceful scene; that the two trappers were just passing on the river, and that the chief was extending a peace pipe toward them. The two women in the upper left quadrant were nomads and they were coming to live in the Indian settlement. The Indian brave under the tree was sitting alone and observing the scene. The patient identified himself with the Indian brave. He said that the Buddha was there because it was a central principal and its purpose was to bring the two races together.

The patient's comment about the buffalo that was hidden from the others was that he hadn't meant to put it there because he was afraid that the buffalo might disturb the peacefulness of the scene but had impulsively placed it there anyway.

Observations

This picture points to several issues that were to be important for the patient. The Indian chief would certainly represent his father complex; the chief of the Indians was the undisputed ruler as was the patient's father. The central position of the Indian chief points to the patient's unconscious identification with his own authoritarian and powerful father.

The nomadic women are anima figures carrying feeling, but they do also point to the nomadic unrooted quality of his feelings. However, they are carrying supplies and coming into the encampment and that is a promising sign.

The hidden buffalo that might disturb the scene represents his own repressed and powerful instincts, as well as his passion and repressed rage which were really cut off and indirectly expressed only in passive-aggressive behavior. The buffalo, the basis of the plains Indians' culture, was a powerful animal in plentiful supply that provided everything necessary for the life and survival of the tribes—milk, meat, fuel, clothing, shelter and transportation (canoes and tents). In short, it was a maternal animal that provided nutrition and shelter. Again, the isolated position of the buffalo points to the cut-off condition of the patient with regard to his own nurturing feminine instincts.

The trappers are hunters who can focus on what they do and are able to move with agility and precision, and who can function under severe conditions. However, these hunters are

in a canoe and on dry sand. A canoe on dry sand can only provide an illusion of movement.

The Buddha derives from the patient's idea of nirvana and
represents a genuine longing and drive to relate to the transpersonal, to integrate the body, mind and spirit since those
were what Buddha represented. However, the East Indian
Buddha, arbitrarily grafted on to this American Indian scene,
in some sense indicates the spiritual drive of this young patient.

It is interesting that in three corners of this picture animals
are hidden away from the view of the human inhabitants,
that is, the buffalo in the lower left quadrant, the horse in the
right lower quadrant, and the two deer in the upper right-hand
corner, underscoring the extent to which his instincts were
repressed. The male and female deer point to a potentiality
for a balanced relationship between the masculine and the
feminine in the patient. The remote position of the two figures,
however, indicates that such a union is a long way off.

The Indian brave sitting deep in the shadow under the tree
on the right, with whom the patient identified, presents a striking image of the isolation of the patient, living deep in his own
shadow, unaware and unable to acknowledge it.

The making of this picture seemed to provide an initiation
into the analytical process. The patient, who had been guarded
in his comments in the previous sessions, quite spontaneously
began to speak about recurring dreams of sacrificing himself
that he had had through most of his life. In the dreams he
had sacrificed himself in order to help others, particularly in
efforts to save women. He remembered one dream in particular
which occurred when he was a teenager and which he remembered vividly because of its nightmarish quality. In the dream
a girl was poised on a cliff and in danger of falling off, and he
was climbing the cliff to help rescue her. He reached her and
in pushing her back fell off himself. The dream indicated a
quite precarious psychological state.

At this point the patient recounted several recurring dreams he had of levitating and of being a great hero who could fly in the manner of Superman.

From then on he was able to work intensively and to begin to look at his shadow. He could speak of his trouble at work and his problem with inertia and passivity. He began to recognize his tendency toward grandiosity and rationalization. He began to recognize his lack of feeling as a problem, and to look at his family and his father in a more objective way.

A month later, he made his second picture.

PICTURE 2

Description

On the left all is in disorder. Many cars are stuck in the sand; a cannon is perched askew on a rock; a tree has fallen. Toward the center on the left are the three monkeys, "See No Evil," "Hear No Evil," "Speak No Evil." A motorcycle rider in the lower left quadrant is also stuck in the sand, as is an army tank.

In the upper left-hand quadrant are a cowboy, a soldier on his stomach shooting at random, a fallen tree and a canal. In the upper right quadrant of the picture, there is a downed airplane, a standing tree and some moss. On the right side is a church with a baby sitting in front of it. In the lower right-hand corner stands a tree.

In the center of the picture is a body of water that the patient called a lake. There is a drowned baby. The seal on the right and the beaver up by the shore, he said, "are doing their own thing." Near the baby are a beached sailboat on a trailer and a child's potty. In the water is the alchemical six-pointed star. The patient spoke of the objects in the water as debris. In the central lower part of the picture are a knight with a spear, some rocks and moss, and a van on top of which stands a man with a television news camera.

2. Progress is Killing Nature

Patient's Comments

"On the left is 'progress,' that is, so-called progress that is killing nature. There's a lot of fighting and destruction." He said the baby in the lake had been a victim and he did not know why, but he felt that this might be the Christ child. He did not speak much about the contents of this picture, but instead spoke about some feelings he had in Central Park a few days earlier. He had walked through the park and had become aware of how beautiful it was. He had gone to the zoo and then was moved to tears by the animals in their cages and felt their separation from nature. He then realized for the first time in his life that it was good to feel, even if one felt sad things, and he had decided not to analyze his feelings that day but just to allow them.

Observations

The work of the past month had been intense and had thrown him into turmoil. This picture is an accurate reflection of his inner state.

This frame of mind is reflected on the left side of the picture where all is in disarray and confusion; where things have come to a standstill. The polluted lake, with a drowned baby, that is full of non-functional rubbish graphically illustrates his stagnated state.

However, there are positive indications also. The first is the penetration to a deeper level. Now there is a clear indication of water, even if polluted, where before there had been only a dry river bed.

The three monkeys symbolize the ancient human unwillingness to recognize or acknowledge evil. Here they probably represent both the patient's *superego* that insisted he must not commit any evil, and his own incapacity to see or deal with his own shadow, which accounted for the paranoid tendency. In addition, the three monkeys represent the cutting off of the three senses that orient us in reality. Here, however, the monkeys are placed in the section of the picture where things are nonfunctional and have come to a standstill. In this context, and when one remembers the work on his shadow in the previous month, it is possible to hope that the attitudes that lay behind the paranoid tendency are becoming nonoperative.

The six-pointed star, that the patient had put into the lake with the other "debris," could be a sign of the spiritual potential of the individual, for it included two interlaced triangles, masculine ($\triangle$) and feminine (∇) which, in alchemy, were called the Sign of Solomon. The six-pointed star was considered an equivalent of the human soul, the conjunction of masculine and feminine, and of fire and water—both pairs being opposites. A hint perhaps of a potentiality for wholeness, lying beside psychological detritus.

The seal and the beaver are both land and water animals, again positive symbols of moving into the depths of the personality. The animals represent instincts that are no longer in a cut-off position.

The church on the right may indicate movement toward a more realistic Western attitude toward the spirit. The baby, with open arms before the church, possibly indicates the potentiality for a new spiritual attitude more native to him. On the other hand, the position of the church, remote from the "action," would indicate separation of his religious orientation from his instincts and what he was feeling.

The crashed plane was reminiscent of the early dreams and fantasies of being a Superman-like hero, flying and levitating above people. It indicated his inner, still unconscious recognition of the bankruptcy of his purely intellectual attitude; a prerequisite for his "coming down to earth" and the quickening of the sensation function.

This picture, so full of fighting and destruction, reminds one of Jung's description of what happens when the fourth function—in this case, sensation—begins to become activated.

> The fourth function is contaminated with the unconscious and, on being made conscious, drags the whole of the unconscious with it. You must then come to terms with the unconscious and try to bring about a synthesis of opposites. At first a violent conflict breaks out . . . Everything in him rises up in revolt and he would defend himself desperately against what looks to him like murderous nonsense" (*CW*, Vol. 12, pp. 152–153, par. 193).

In general, the nonfunctional quality of the picture reflects his problems with the workaday world, which were pushing him toward recognition of the bankruptcy of his value system.

The patient was moving toward realization that the civilization and materialism, of which he was so critical because it was destroying nature, had arisen precisely out of his own kind of identification with the intellect. Just as thinking divorced from feeling was destroying the ecology of the world, so it was harming him.

The man with the TV news camera may reflect either his *conscious* attitude of detached, observing noninvolvement, or perhaps a potentiality for a new kind of objective recording of inner and outer events, in the same sense that the sandplay process is photographed and studied, for the sake of meaning.

The next picture was made a month later.

PICTURE 3

Description

On the upper right is a shed or barn with a small calf or cow in front of it. There are trees and moss and acorns all over the picture and some rocks. Near the water, on the right-hand side of the picture, is a playful horse.

On the left-hand side of the picture is a giraffe, a white elephant, and a gazelle in the far, upper-left corner. In the center area, near some flowering trees, is a black gorilla. A piece of brain coral lies near the center on the left.

Patient's Comments

The patient called his picture a farm and said the following:

> *The white elephant, he said, is peaceful, loyal, calm; it has no natural enemies. It is concerned with its group. It would like to be a mate for life.*

> *The gazelle is vulnerable, defensive. When one is vulnerable, one needs defenses. The gazelle's chief defense is to be able to run away quickly.*

> *The gorilla is closer to man than the other animals: it is a vegetarian and it, too, would mate for life.*

He put in the playful horse because, he said, he liked it.

He said he made this picture to calm himself because he had been in a great deal of turmoil. He was feeling quite angry with his father, but still unable to confront the anger or express it directly to his father.

On the evening before he made this picture, he and his girl-friend had admitted their need for each other, and this had put him into intense perturbation since his ideal had been not to need anyone or to be needed. This capacity to experience need and to express it had pleased him, but had also frightened him because he still was unprepared for feeling and fearful of commitment. At the same time, he was able to explain to her his need for solitude because, he reported, she had previously interpreted his need as rejection of her.

At this time he wrote a poem, the first line of which was "The pink dawn steals over the father's shadow."

Observations

A month had elapsed between the last picture and this one.

Although he called this the farm, it seemed to have a feeling like the Garden of Eden.

The three animals "who mate for life" on the left side of the picture seem to point to a potentiality for commitment that was developing in the patient. On the other hand, the fact that they are single animals—one of each—signified that there is still much solitary feeling and loneliness. The Garden, however, is providing a meeting place for each of those lonely animals, indicating that he was moving toward consciousness of what the solitary animals represented within him. All the animals are herbivorous, which suggests that the vegetative-animal level of the unconscious has been touched. The absence of humans also suggests this deep level of the unconcscious.

The brain coral, which looks very much like an ossified brain, would seem to point to the drying up of the purely intellectual point of view.

The gazelle, or deer, has tradionally been an anima-soul prefiguration.

3. The Pink Dawn

For the next three months, the patient made no more sand pictures because a large amount of dream material that needed interpretation and integration began to emerge. In addition, because he was now much involved in the reality of his every-day life there was a great deal to talk about and to deal with, and he became less interested in making the pictures.

During that time, his work improved a great deal, and he was relieved about that. He continued to struggle with the feeling of anger with his father whom he still addressed as "sir."

He was also struggling with his feelings about his relation-ship with the girlfriend. It seemed that the closer he came to being able to make a commitment, the more unhappy and demanding she became. He reported that nothing he did was good enough in her eyes. He felt that she was self-absorbed and that she was not really trying to meet his needs, but kept insisting that he was not meeting hers. In short, he was begin-ning to see her shadow and to recognize and accept his own needs.

At about this time, his work had improved to such an extent that he was given a coveted assignment in another city. Before leaving for what was to be a five-month period in that city, he made the next picture.

PICTURE 4

Description

The patient called this an absurd picture. He said, "It is a surreal inversion." The idea was that nothing was used as it was meant to be. In the upper-center of the picture is a totem pole which dominates the scene. In front of the totem is an overturned butter churn and a pine cone. In the upper left-hand corner there is a mountain on which is a red coral. This was to symbolize absurdity in the sense that a red coral should be in the water, but instead it was on top of a mountain. The right-hand upper quadrant contains a round adobe house, and on it sits a crowned frog.

The lower half of the picture contains a body of water with a canal going off to the lower-left quadrant. In that body of water is a skull, a clock turned over on its side, a sand island, and on the shore is an overturned vase. On the left-hand side of the picture, the figure of a Chinese boy is turned upside-down with his head in the sand. On the right-hand side, near the water, is a figure of a vulture, a bird on a brown barren tree.

Patient's Comments

The patient said that he had chosen these objects at random. He did not have much comment to make on them. He said that the butter churn was early American and that it indicated something "going back to the land." He said the bird on the tree was a vulture which eats dead bodies. He put the crowned frog on the adobe house for fun, and the clock on its side represented the element of time. He said that the upside-down boy was the way he had been living life, with his head in the sand.

Observations

The patient's functioning had improved noticeably. But he was struggling a lot during this period of transition. He was trying to come to grips with his shadow for the first time and to find his own values as distinct from his father's. He was engaging in a new and often painful attempt to relate to his girl-friend. He was in constant struggle to discover, define and express his feelings. In addition, all of his previously held assumptions were now in serious question. He was suffering a profound change in his entire value system. Things were indeed not what they had appeared to be, and this picture reflected that truth.

However, the picture also points to an emerging and increasing feminine presence in the patient's psyche. The butter churn represents a traditionally feminine mode of coagulation or solidification. The redness of the coral points to passion and blood. The vase is certainly a feminine container.

4. A Surreal Inversion

The vulture, as a devourer of the dead, was sacred to most of the great goddesses, Hathor, Nekhbet, Maat, Isis and Hera. Believed to be a compassionate purifier since it did not devour any living things, the vulture was perhaps after his old values.

The clock, although on its side, represented his increasing ability to live in concrete reality. He was, in fact, acceding to the requirements of linear time. He was prompt for business, social and analytical appointments and he was budgeting his work time much more productively.

As an emblem of man's mortality, the skull also indicated the patient's new awareness of time, pointing as well to further desiccation of the patient's one-sided and intellectual orientation. The skull if also the symbol of indestructibility and immortality; that which survives after the body has been destroyed. In alchemy, it was seen as a receptacle for life and thought, a vessel of transformation.

The whole picture is overseen by the Indian totem. The totem, representing the animal as mythical ancestor and protector, might here be suggesting a spiritual potentiality based on the patient's own instincts. His calling the totem evil would indicate his ambivalence toward his instincts, or to change.

The frog is a quintessential animal of transformation, living in the water and then on land, changing form from tadpole to frog, and mythically, changing from a prince to frog, to prince again.

So one could say of this picture that although the patient was confused and often in pain, the struggle was in the service of transformation. The patient returned after several months of work in another city and made the following picture:

PICTURE 5

Description

Here, after a five-month interruption, the picture is similar to the previous one, in that objects are used arbitrarily, not in their usual functional sense.

When the patient first made this picture, the objects were used functionally and were fairly well evenly distributed, but it didn't please him so he simply picked up the objects that had been on the left side and moved everything tightly into the right side of the picture, leaving the left-lower quadrant empty.

In the lower right-hand corner, a wineglass is overturned, a bridge stands on its end, a chair is upside down, two clay modeling instruments are simply stuck into the ground. Near some moss a caricature of a Stone Age Viking is overturned and half buried in the sand. Moving upward from the right-

5. The Shrine of What Is

hand corner, there is a representation of a primitive phallic god that has fallen. Above that is a dark, small figure of a Chinese monk upside down with his head in the sand.

Above that is a crescent-shaped tray that is standing on its side. In the center, at the top of the picture, is a flat stone and between the stone and the upturned crescent is a small wooden bridge. Below that are some pine cones.

To the left of the flat stone is a round adobe house that has been turned on its side and thrust into the ground to make a kind of cave-like structure. Above it are two clay modeling instruments thrust into the sand.

A black and white stone and some moss are in the water and slightly to the right of the moss and the water is an over-turned house. Close to that is a round adobe disc which is in the sand.

Patient's Comments

I used these figures and things abstractly. Nothing has its normal meaning. I don't know what meaning most of it has at all. The whole thing is a temple of what is. The crescent is a shrine. It is the shrine of what is, and what is, is not what it appears to be. It's all inexpressible and difficult to comprehend."

Observations

During his time away, the patient had been struggling with key issues of his individual relationship to concrete reality, i.e., achievement in the collective as prescribed by his father versus his own idealogical and emotional resistance to it; his identification with the intellect versus his innate powerful feelings and instincts. He struggled with his need for perfection which, derived from his rigid background, fueled his obsessive-compulsive tendencies and his fear of commitment.

The similarity of this picture with the last picture he made before leaving indicates that he was still struggling with the same conflicts.

Moving everything to the right side of the sand tray and the meaningless arbitrary use of objects reflect his growing unease with his unsuccessful efforts to manipulate reality to fit his own confused conceptions. However, that stress, I believe, arose out of his growing awareness that he was approaching a point of no return; that is, that he could not go on with his old orientation and that he did not yet know what the new one would be, nor what its implication would be for his life.

The hopeful indications were that although he had been away and had had no outer support (and there had been some

regression in his work habits), he was no longer smoking marijuana during working hours and had cut down smoking in
general, and he managed a reasonable level of productivity.
Also, he was able to engage more freely in an emotional way
with his girlfriend who spent weekends with him. He no longer
deferred to her as an authority on feelings and relationship,
and he tried not to withdraw when there was a disagreement.
He was also more able to reveal his vulnerability to her.

There are several interesting features in this picture. The
clearing of the lower-left third of the picture, the area most
associated with the unconscious, leaves room for something
new to occur.

The clay tools represent work with the earth principle,
reality and the instincts.

The Chinese man with his head in the sand is placed in front
of the upended crescent-shaped shrine, which suggests a feminine crescent moon. In fact, the upended male is dwarfed by
this feminine shape. Noteworthy here, too, is the fact that
the upended boy in the previous picture and the man in this
picture are both Asian, which might be alluding to the demise
of the patient's purely intellectual identification with Asian
philosophies and the pursuit of nirvana.

It is interesting that there is a bridge, virtually the only
object used functionally, between the crescent shrine and the
flat rock. The shape of the rock suggests a platform, a potential
new standpoint. The implication is that the feminine value and
presence within him may enable a transition to a new more
firmly grounded standpoint.

The man-made house is overturned. Perhaps a new organic
shelter may arise.

The mandala-like disc near the center of the picture suggests
a potentiality for centering.

The most striking feature of the picture, however, is the
fall of the primitive male phallic god, which suggests the potential resolution of his father complex and the end of the patriar-

chal identification. In archetypal terms, it points to the death
of the "old king," the sacrifice of the old supreme value that
opens the way for the new, and, in fact, the fallen phallic god
lies before the feminine crescent moon. When the new moon
rises, the old king dies.

There were no new sand pictures for the next five months
because he did not wish to make any. No interpretive connection was made between the fallen phallic god and the archetypal or personal father, since that would have hindered the
autonomous unconscious process. However, he seemed to
know instinctively that he needed more conscious understanding and consolidation of what was happening to him.

During the ensuing period he was able to experience his
feelings of rage against his father and to resolve his father
complex to a considerable extent, as Picture 5 had indicated.
He was more able to accept a less than perfect self-image and
to cope with his father in a new way. Some *three months
after* making the last picture, he dreamed of weeping while
his father lay dying in his arms and there was a reconciliation
between them. He was able to say at this time, "A life devoted
to the mind pulls you to abstractions too soon."

At a certain point during this period, he had a dream of
witnessing his girlfriend in bed with another man, of feeling
helpless and paralyzed because of his fear of losing her. His
girlfriend had, in fact, threatened to leave him on several
occasions, insisting that he was still not "meeting her emotional needs." After this dream, he was able to feel more
clearly his own suffering in the relationship, and he allowed
his own anger with her. He began to see her shadow and to
feel that she was "self-absorbed" and essentially unable to hear
or respond to his newfound and experienced needs and vulnerability.

He began to write poetry frequently. In one poem addressed
to her, he wrote, "If what I am is not sufficient for you, then
I am not sufficient, and I will not try to become sufficient."

Despite the withdrawal of his projections and the difficulties in their relationship, he began to feel there might be a better chance to work things out if they made a mutual commitment to each other.

Although he had given up marijuana, except for rare occasions, and his work patterns had stabilized, he had come to the conclusion that he really didn't like his job or living in the city. He discussed this with his girlfriend and told her he would like to find a different kind of job in his field and to move to a western part of the United States which they both loved. He asked her to marry him and to go with him. She agreed, in principle. He made active efforts but when he did in fact find such a job, she found herself unable to make the commitment she had so long insisted on from him.

There began what was to be a drawn out and painful effort to save their relationship with several episodes of breaking off and reconciliation. He suffered much anguish and there were many tears. The worst was over when one day he could say, "Pain doesn't kill."

He accepted the new job anyway and there remained three more months in which to try to work out their problems before his departure. He spontaneously began to make sand pictures again, in fact, making one at almost every session. From this point on, as he struggled to define himself within the troubled relationship, the emergence and differentiation of his own feminine nature, as well as a new instinctually related spirituality, became increasingly apparent in the sand pictures.

PICTURE 6

Description

This picture is divided into two main land masses connected in the center by a large flat stone which acts as a platform or a bridge between the two land masses.

On it stands a blue dwarf playing a drum. In front of the dwarf is a black stone. On the left side of the stone is a bridge that stands on its side acting as a ladder, and reaching down into the water.

In the right lower quadrant, below the stone, there is a stylized aluminum elephant which the patient called a "silver" elephant. On the water, in the lower right-hand corner of the quadrant, is another blue dwarf on a raft.

In the upper right-hand quadrant is the same disc that appeared in the center of the last picture. Above it, barely visible, but at the very edge of the right-hand margin of the picture, is another "silver" elephant. Above that, slightly to the left, still in the upper right-hand quadrant, one can barely discern something coming through a sand mound that is a buried wooden egg.

In the upper center is a small ring of sea glass in the water. Moving to the left, to the upper left-hand quadrant, there are three rocks. Two of them are semiprecious stones.

At the left-hand border of the picture is a piece of sea glass that has the form of a question mark.

Below that, at the lower left-hand corner, is a platform that bridges the lower corner of the tray, and on the platform is a dolphin (not visible in this picture). Moving to the right in the lower left-hand quadrant, there is an oil lamp in the sand and a cone-shaped dome on its side and another piece of sea glass in the shape of a question mark.

Patient's Comments

The patient said that the picture felt like the religious Stonehenge scene in the motion picture *2001*. He said that the film appealed to something that was true. It said yes to the origin, the source of things. The stones and objects were part of Stonehenge.

He said that in the lower right-hand quadrant, the blue dwarf standing on a ferry with no tiller was bewildered and scared and didn't know where he was going or "what it was all about." He was drifting with the tide. The dwarf with the

6. Yes to the Origin

drum was an agent of a sinister force that he did not comprehend, but also a herald announcing something new. The black
stone had magical power.

The upended bridge standing in the water was a means of
getting down to the water. He stated that he liked water, that
he usually felt secure in it.

The dolphin on the platform was part of the picture but
somewhat removed because it brought a different perspective,
an observer status. He said it was important that it not be
human; it should be a symbol of removed understanding and
perspective that couldn't be embodied in the human figure.

The round platform in the upper right-hand quadrant was a religious circle acting as another bridge, but he didn't know to where.

The elephants were an elemental life force.

About the egg buried in the upper right-hand quadrant, he said, "Something is being born. Something has to be discovered and uncovered."

Observations

In this picture several new developments have followed after "the fall of the old king."

In the lower left quadrant that had been deliberately emptied in the last picture (5), there now lies an oil lamp, a potentiality for new illumination or consciousness. On that same corner sits a dolphin surveying the scene.

The dolphin carries an implication of an observing instinctual and guiding intelligence of playfulness, swiftness and loyalty. A transitional animal, a mammal highly adapted to life in the water with a very high intelligence and possibly primitive language, it is an allegory for salvation, serving in myths and legends as a savior of mariners and children, either by leading or carrying them. It is the steed of gods, goddesses and humans: Poseidon, Ino, Leto, Thetis, and particularly Eros, the god of love and relatedness. It is sacred to the moon goddess.

The dolphin probably represents the granting of the capacity for intelligence to an instinct. Its elevated position also suggests the granting of status and objectivity to instinct. It is on the scene, but still on the periphery.

The solitary elephant of an earlier picture (3) now has a partner. The elephant alone of all the large animals is capable of having its tremendous strength and energy put to creative human use. It is an instinct that allows itself to be guided. Like the dolphin, it is the mount of deities and kings.

Several characteristics of the elephant are relevant to the patient's psychological state. It is a particularly "committed" socialized herd animal. The herd will protect its wounded and dying and will make efforts to free trapped members. Female elephants act as midwives for mothers who are giving birth and will remain with the mother until the young can join the herd. The herd is led by an experienced female elephant (*Larousse,* p. 581).

The glass question marks reflect an open, questioning attitude as opposed to the previously held closed certainties.

The partially buried egg points to the possibility of the birth of a new point of view.

The stone platform, now enlarged and in the center, suggests a coagulating-centering process that was merely hinted at in the last picture. The upper and lower land masses are connected, a potential connection perhaps of two parts of reality, perhaps masculine and feminine.

The platform is a natural stone. Many primitive deities were said to have been born of stone. Christ was the stone on whom the godless would fall (*Luke* 20, 18), and the cornerstone rejected by the builder.

The black stone on the platform hints at the "all" of the alchemical prima materia, or possibly the philosopher's stone that held magical power or transformative energy.

All of the above hint at a possible constellation of the Self.

The blue dwarfs suggest the Cabiri, the magical wonder workers of the great goddess, her creative phallic aspects. Of the Cabiri, Jung said, "In the form of the dactyls, they are also the gods of invention, small and apparently insignificant, like impulses of the unconscious, but endowed with the same mighty power" (*CW,* Vol. 12, p. 157, par. 203). The dwarfs point to the creative activation of the feminine-matriarchal unconscious now that the "old king" attitude has fallen.

The blue dwarf on the center connecting platform, whom the patient described as both "an agent of a sinister force" and "a herald of something new," might well be his newly activated positive shadow elements, namely his new capacities to feel and express anger, and to hold to his own standpoint which is what one does on a platform. His new ability to own his own negative feelings, to "beat his own drum" was really enabling him to connect and relate in a new way to the meaningful others in his life, including his father, his woman friend, his boss, and, for the first time, his mother.

The blue dwarf on the ferry that is just drifting is a harbinger of a new ego. The figure is to recur in several pictures that follow.

The bridge going down to the water, in congruence with the stone platform, forms a cave-like structure that might harbor the drifting ferry and perhaps mark an end to the patient's unfocused wanderings. While it is true that the boat is drifting and without an ego steering it, there is a sense of water moving and a tide that is taking the raft to a safe shelter.

Referring to dwarfs, Jung remarks.

> They stand in grotesque contrast to the heavenly gods and poke fun at them. Originating in the dark, they are intensely striving from the depths to the heights and are therefore always to be found both below and above . . . [they are] obviously an unconscious content struggling toward the light . . . what I have elsewhere called "the treasure hard to obtain" (*CW,* Vol. 12, p. 158, par. 204).

When one thinks of these blue dwarfs in the context of the above paragraph, plus the emergence of the mysterious egg, it is possible to consider them as coagulating elements of a newly constellating activated Self.

PICTURE 7

Description

A central mountain. In the center of the mountain is a crater and in it an uncovered green egg. Starting at the top of the mountain and going clockwise: A dozing Mexican at the lip of the crater. Below, on the outer side of the mountain, is a figure of a Chinese monk in a recess in the mountainside. To the right, a black knight wearing a red helmet with a sword in hand is trying to slash at a green frog. Still moving clockwise, on the right side of the mountain are a black boy, a scarecrow facing outward, and below it, a kneeling man.

Moving further clockwise is a monk in a red robe; above him an infant lies in an alcove.

To the left, at the lip of the crater, stands a devil overlooking the egg, and behind the devil stands an angel. Below the angel, to the left, is a coffee grinder.

Further on (on the left side of the mountain), in a recess, are the three "Speak, See and Hear No Evil" monkeys.

Moving toward a full circle, below the dozing Mexican, is a mouse and a skull.

In the upper right-hand corner of the sand tray are two large rocks through which comes a tiny wayfarer on a tiny raft.

In the lower left-hand corner, two tiny peasant figures work the land.

Patient's Comments

This picture is about the search for the Holy Grail, which is the egg. The red monk on the right is very serious and determined, but he is approaching it frontally and that's probably not the way. He will have a hard long climb.

The Mexican is very near to it but he is not really trying.

The man kneeling on the right is humble and he is going to follow a path around the bottom of the mountain and spiral up. He, in a way, is going toward something by seemingly going away from it.

The baby in the hole is innocence. It has its own nearness to the Grail, but it is still separate from it. With experience it may get to it.

The black boy is hitchhiking. He won't make it. He's not relying on his own power.

The devil is there, but he can't get into it.

The monkeys have gone as far as they can go.
The black knight warrior constructs impediments so he can fight through them. A frog is an absurd obstacle to kill.
The skull is the sign of our mortality. It laughs at our absurdities.
The Chinese Buddhist monk, sitting in the back recess looking out to the ocean, is a pretender.
The scarecrow is there to fend off those who would be easily discouraged.
The boatman coming in from the upper-right is too preoccupied with physical reality to focus on the Grail. He may be taking the shortest route of all. The same is true for the farmhands.
The angel is just too beautiful to be real.
What they are all seeking won't be the end, but just a beginning.

Observations

Here, with the mountain, we have the centering that was presaged by the disc in Picture 5 and the stone platform in Picture 6. There is a coming together here and potential integration of various relevant issues in this process, a kind of summarizing progress report. The now green (fertile) egg is fully disclosed, although not easily accessible, in the stable mountain.

The mouse would represent the patient's remaining tendency for gnawing obsessive compulsivity.

His comments about the skull would indicate an existential awareness of mortality, of the limitation of physical human life, and a growing acceptance of the limitations of spatio-temporal reality.

The sleeping Mexican represents the patient's own tendency to passivity.

His comments about the three monkeys being stuck and going nowhere point, perhaps, to his having gone beyond his previous state of unconsciousness. And it may well be that the "paranoid" tendency has been arrested.

The black knight reflects the remaining aggressive rigidity that would destroy the transformative power of the green frog.

7. The Search for the Holy Grail

The monk looking out to sea represents the remains of his inflated nirvana ambitions. His comments indicate recognition of the inauthenticity of that ambition. The man on his knees, in the traditional position of the penitent, circling the base of the mountain, perhaps signals the end of his grandiosity and his genuine longing and willingness to struggle for spiritual meaning.

The black boy who is hitchhiking is a symbol for his shadow tendency to find an easy way.

The now alive and innocent infant is, in a sense, a resurrection of the infant who had been drowned in the second picture. As such, it represents a potentiality for a new, saving spiritual consciousness, although there is not yet a real concept of the Grail.

The devil figure, the dark adversary of God, could represent intellectual doubt about what the patient was experiencing and also his power shadow, the will to power of the Ego, to which the Grail would indeed be inaccessible.

His comments about the idealized angel figure may also be alluding to his more realistic image of the feminine. At this time he was seeing both his woman friend and his mother in a more three-dimensional view, including shadow and light.

The peasants working in the lower-left corner (an area representing the instincts and the unconscious) quietly till the soil, unconscious of the significance of the scene around them. From the opposite corner (area of intellect and consciousness) comes the tiny wayfarer, also absorbed in his activity, possibly representing a new consciousness. The patient, in fact, was beginning to sense that only through his struggle with day-to-day reality and the darkness within his being could he hope to be touched by the transpersonal.

The contents of both corners represent the patient's growing capacity to function productively in sensate reality in linear time.

One remaining observation remains to be made. Looked at from a different perspective, one can discern this mountain as a head, or perhaps the head of an owl, the two recesses being seen as eyes. With this point of view, the green egg lies where the brain would be. Perhaps a new brain is forming, with a new way of thinking and a new way to the spirit. It may be no accident that in the center now is the egg, called the Holy Grail, the quintessential feminine container of the spirit. The Grail symbol lies in a central mountain accessible from opposite directions, from the land and from the sea.

Within a day or two after making this picture, the patient, while relating more directly and openly with his friend, was now able to assert and define his need for separateness and time for himself which had not previously been the case. He was no longer willing to accept her authority nor to try to relate to his friend on her terms exclusively. Their struggle continued.

PICTURE 8

Description

In the center of this picture is a windmill and beside it a rock.

In the lower-left quadrant are bushes and pine cones through which a lion emerges.

In the upper-left quadrant are small acorns and a sign desig-nating someone's name and residence. There are three rows of cultivated flowers in the midst of which is a mouse.

In the upper-center is a crashed plane and a fat man waving his arms facing the plane.

On the right side is a body of water with some trees and bushes around it and a five-pointed star figure in the center. Above the five-pointed star figure a crocodile is emerging from the water. On the opposite lower shore, on the right side, are a pelican and stork.

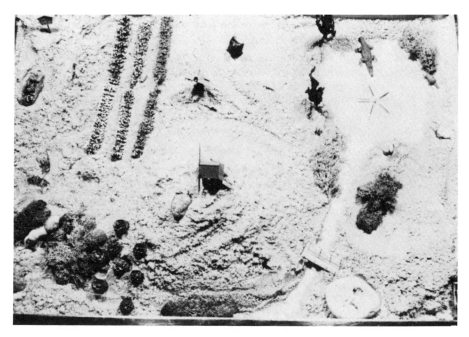

8. The Raving Fat Man

A canal or stream of water flows from the body of water. On either side of the canal is a hill; on the left side stands the windmill and on the hill on the right are some bushes. A bridge crosses the canal connecting the two sides. Below is a flat rock, again suggesting a platform.

In the lower right-hand corner, not clearly discernible in the picture, stands the Empire State Building.

Patient's Comments

The lion stalking the mouse is absurd.

The crashed jet plane is half-buried in the sand. It is antitechnology asserting itself. The fat man is ranting at nothing. There is

*no one to hear. He is a crazy man and he is shrieking that technol-
ogy has destroyed the countryside. He is a madman who feels he is
going to lead a crusade to raze all that man has created. Nothing
man has created is worth saving in his eyes! He is obsessed.*

The patient sat silently for quite a while and then he said in
a very quiet voice, "I have been extremely rigid and self-
righteous. Outwardly, I pretended to be reasonable, but inwardly I was not. I was absolutist about a lot of things. I
thought I could do anything and everything, that I would lead
the world on a crusade away from its problems. I would start
with this country by getting into politics and then I would
save the world. I was the raving, ranting fat man."

Observations

The crashed plane, the raving man, the patient's comments
about them and, most importantly, his revealing his most grandiose ambitions and his recognition of their delusionary quality,
indicate the resolution of his paranoid-megalomanic inflation
and the remnants of his father complex.

The windmill at the center of the picture, a man-made yet
natural means of transforming energy, harnesses the wild
masculine energy of the wind (spirit) to grind the feminine
corn (earth) so that it can be ingested and integrated. The
windmill can therefore be seen as a symbol of the union of
opposites of masculine and feminine elements.

The windmill may be the new response to the crashed plane,
or perhaps results from the transformation of the inflated and
paranoid attitude.

The patient's being able to call absurd the stalking of the
mouse by the lion, the king of the beasts, is another indication
of a more realistic posture since the patient in this case identifies with neither the lion (the male aggressor) nor the mouse
(the victim).

On the other hand, one can't help feeling that there is something positive about the wild beast with its primitive energy

stalking, and perhaps putting an end to, the nagging, gnawing little beast that could symbolize the patient's obsessive-compulsive pattern.

The emergence of differentiation between the masculine and the feminine is suggested in this picture by the domination of the left side of the picture by the lion and the almost totally feminine character of the right side.

On the right, the body of water bears a striking resemblance either to a uterus and birth canal, or a head and gullet with a breast on either side.

On the upper shore of the water is an emerging crocodile, a symbol of the cold-blooded devouring mother. It is also a transitional animal; its natural habitats are land and water.

On the opposite shore is a pelican, the symbolic opposite of the crocodile, since it is a symbol of the archetypal nourishing mother. According to legend, it feeds its young on its own blood by pecking open its own breast (*Dictionary of Symbols*, p. 240). The appearance of the pelican here indicates the potential healing of the mother image. Jung refers to the pelican nourishing its young with its own blood as an allegory of Christ (*CW*, Vol. 12, Fig. 189, p. 184).

Between the opposite aspects of the mother lies the five-pointed star figure. Jung points out that the five-pointed star symbolizes material, sensate man (*CW*, Vol. 9, Part I, p. 373, par. 680).

The number 5 also represents the quintessence, which Jung elsewhere refers to as "the equivalent of aether, the finest and most subtle substance" (*CW*, Vol. 14, p. 322, par. 450).

Paracelsus called the fifth essence the spirit of truth, stating that it was incomprehensible without the inspiration of the Holy Ghost (*CW*, Vol. 13, p. 130, par. 166).

Perhaps, then, the implication here is that the reconciliation between the devouring and nourishing aspects of the feminine, for this patient, will require both the material and spiritual spheres.

Finally, the bridge connects the area where stands the Empire State Building, a symbol of man's intellectual and technological achievement, with the natural windmill, the symbol of man's harmonious connection with nature.

If one looks in a diagonal line from the lower-right through the center to the upper left-hand corner, one sees a straight line connecting the Empire State Building (material) to the windmill (spiritual), to the sign announcing a residence and the name of the owner, suggesting the emergence of a defined ego identity, and the structure in which it lives.

The patient at this time was writing poetry regularly. His effort to relate to his friend and at the same time maintain his own position is expressed in the following lines from one poem:

> It's so much easier to love
> When you don't ask me,
> To demand is to have robbed
> The giver of his pleasure.

PICTURE 9

Description

Here the differentiation and connection between the masculine and feminine emerge more clearly. In the center, a system of earthworks and waterways and rocks that the patient called a mysterious design separates two hilly sides.

The left side is now almost entirely devoted to feminine symbols. The right side is masculine. Both sides are dominated by large circular mirrors that face each other. Behind the mirrors are large rocks anchoring a red string that bisects the picture horizontally. From the string in the center hangs a devil that dominates the whole picture.

On the right masculine side, from the top downward, is a bald-headed professor type. Just below him, Evel Knievel on a motorcycle has fallen off a catapult. Nearby a crusader stands, sword in hand. To the far right, above the rock, is a "silver" elephant. Toward the water, with his back to the mirror, sits a meditating Chinese monk. Below the rock stands the primitive phallic god once again; a soldier with a bazooka stands in front of it. Below him a knight with spear at the ready rides forward on a black horse. Nearby a rickshaw with a male passenger is overturned; a man with two guns faces toward the other mountain.

At the bottom of the picture, closest to the water, the blue dwarf is gazing across at the other side.

On the left, feminine figures more or less balance those on the masculine side.

In the lower left quadrant, stands a white Kwan Yin figure (goddess of mercy). Slightly above is a rickshaw with occupant which has been overturned. Just below the upended rock on the left, is a "silver" elephant to balance the one on the right side. An angel kneels in front of the mirror. A ballet dancer in red, closest to the water on this side, faces toward a blue dwarf. Behind her stands a wolf covered by a sheep.

Toward the upper left-hand corner are two peasant women. In the uppermost left corner are several large snakes in a pit. Behind the mirror on the left-hand side and balancing the phallic god, on the right side, stands a large totem.

Patient's Comments

Between the two mounds is a mysterious design. The mounds represent the two sides of what is. The right side is masculine, the left is feminine. The two sides are trying to approach each other.

The devil in the center is part of the perception each side has of the other. The two mirrors reflect each other's perception of the other. Maybe the mirrors represent the rigid ways of thinking of both sides.

There are opposing totems. The father-god on the right and the totem on the left.

The snakes (the upper left-hand corner) are the hidden dangers on the women's side.

The "silver" elephants are the elemental life force on both sides.

The wolf in sheep's clothing is the inner aggression in women that gives rise to male fear of what is underneath.

The rickshaws are overturned because they had people in them who wanted an easy journey, who wanted to use other people's strength to get somewhere.

The Chinese woman (Kwan Yin) is the pious female counterpart to the praying Buddhist on the other side.

The kneeling angel is a reformed siren.

The bald-headed professor is giving a lecture on the aspects of women. Nobody is listening.

The blue dwarf is bewildered and scared. But he is coming closest to getting someplace. He is receptive, rather than ready to do battle.

The ballet dancer is concentrating on her art, on what she is doing. She's the most feminine and the most advanced of all.

Observations

It is not difficult to discern the suggestion of an image of Zeus in the "mysterious design" in the center. It has a rather wrathful aspect which is to be expected since it is formed where the water and earth are intermingled, where the earth is emerging from the water; at a very primitive level of the psyche. (If one accepts the notion that the patient's devouring father was a modern-day Kronus, then the appearance of Zeus in the patient's sand picture is quite startling, since Zeus was the son of Kronus. It should be remembered that the patient knew nothing of the Kronus amplification. In fact, the patient did not perceive the Zeus image until it was pointed out to him when the slides were shown at a later date.)

It appears to be the emergence of the masculine spirit out of the native instinctual matriarchal depths of the patient's psyche. In psychological terms, it hints at an early coagulation of the patriarchal level of development as the rudimentary new

9. A Mysterious Design

ego (the blue dwarf) is appearing; as postulated by Neumann.

Another feature of the picture is the patient's effort to balance both sides: the totems on either side, the "silver" elephants on either side, the fallen rickshaws, the ballet dancer and the blue dwarf, the mirrors and rocks balancing each other, the red string that connects the two sides. (Different colored strings were available to the patient; he deliberately chose red.)

The different aspects of the two genders as depicted in this picture indicate the growing complexity and richness of the patient's perceptions of the masculine and feminine, and his struggle to integrate them.

As for the angel who was formerly a siren, mythological sirens sang songs of such sweetness as to lure mariners to their doom; psychologically, to be lost or imprisoned in the unconscious. Angels were forces or powers ascending and descending between the realm of the spirit and world of phenomena. They were generally believed to carry a divine message or inspiration.

So here we have some sign of the transformation of the feminine and/or unconscious from a threatening to a helpful aspect; from the demonic to the divine.

The patient's characterization of the feminine ballet dancer as the most advanced of all indicates a progression in his own anima development and his growing capacity to exist in spatio-temporal time. In Hindu belief, the dance of Shiva symbolically created the union of space and time which resulted in the creation of the phenomenal world. Dance is a form of creation and incarnation of energy, an ancient form of magic and transformation. Specifically, it is a physical and dynamic means of stimulating, organizing and expressing emotion. And in reality, the patient was now capable of expressing his feelings more clearly and directly.

The meaning of the figure of the devil may be quite complex.

The patient's characterization of the devil as a projection by both sides implies his acknowledgment that he had a shadow to project.

The hanging of the devil between the masculine and feminine sides might be some precognition he had of the possibility of the relationship not working.

The devil may have represented the emotional ordeal he was undergoing as he gained consciousness of the destructive mutual projections in the relationship and his growing bafflement and pain in it.

The devil may also have represented his own dark side, which was manifesting overtly, signaling the end of his identification with goodness and "noblesse oblige." Shortly thereafter he did express his rage and frustration and forced a rupture of the relationship.

Although very sad, he weathered the break well. He continued to work productively and saw friends.

There remains the question of the two mirrors. Why two? Was it an attempt to differentiate masculine and feminine consciousness or did the two mirrors represent his tendency to paranoid obsessive ideation?

Two mirrors enable one to see behind oneself, that is, to see one's own shadow. They could represent a thrust toward increased consciousness or an obsessive looking behind one's shoulder. Double mirrors suggest an attempt to see infinity, yet it is an illusionary infinity, for two mirrors facing each other simply reflect each other. The question here remains open.

PICTURE 10

Description
Here again is a masculine-feminine division. Two mountains are separated by a narrow body of water; the left side holds feminine symbols, the right, masculine. A bridge extends halfway across.

On the top of the mountain on the left stands a miniature trophy cup, called a chalice by the patient. In it he has put a small red gemstone. In front of the victory trophy is a ladybug and a polished blue stone wrapped in red string. Behind the mountain, two peasants till the soil. Some pine cones, sea glass and moss are scattered about. At the base near the water stands a herald facing the other side.

10. The Toilers in the Field

The mountain on the right has a beach with sea glass, a vulture on a tree, and two knights fighting each other.

At the pinnacle of this mountain is a large mirror. The professor who had been expounding on the qualities of women in the last picture (9) is now upended in front of the mirror with his head in the sand.

A Union soldier with a gun stands in front of the mirror. Behind the mirror is a skull.

At the base of the mountain down near the water stands the blue dwarf. Just before him stands a torii, which would ordinarily serve as a gateway to a Shinto temple in Japan. Before it is a sign with Asian writing on it.

In the upper right-hand corner lies the Mexican floating on the water; around him are three dolphins.

The red thread that is wrapped around the stone in the upper left quadrant extends diagonally across the sand tray and is anchored on the *outside* of the lower right corner by a tiny baboon (picture 10A).

Patient's Comments

The left side is the sought-after place. The chalice is really the goal. It may look like the peak, but it is really only the beginning. It contains an egg, or gem, which would be the next step.

The baboon climbing up from the outside on the right is holding the string and climbing on it. It is the string that connects everything. The baboon has the longest and most difficult route to go, but he is on the most direct line.

On the mountain on the right, the men are questing, but the crusade doesn't lead anywhere.

The mirror reflects light across to the other mountain so that one can see on the left side better than without the mirror. In a sense one can see farther by reflected light.

The skull behind the mirror is kind of an aspect that one can't see. Maybe it's in the unconscious. The crusaders are not in touch with the negative aspects of their questing life on the hill. That's

10a. Detail.

what the skull stands for. The vulture represents a warning of danger.

My friend the dwarf is looking longingly across at the left mountain. There are heiroglyphs on the sign which tell how to complete the bridge, but he can't read them.

The herald is trying to tell people how to come over.

The upside-down professor in front of the mirror with his head in the sand is expounding and intellectualizing. His head is really in the sand; maybe that's where his head always was.

The toilers in the field, in the upper left-hand corner, in the valley, are hidden and protected from the Crusaders. They are working quietly in the fields, not just sitting back.

Observations

The patient's comments, I believe, accurately describe his state at the time and the aptness of his remarks indicates his growing connection with the inner and outer world.

He repeats here again that goal, this time the chalice, is only a beginning. Here is the suggestion of an individuation process —the path with no final goal, only new beginnings. The chalice is another intimation of the constellation of the Self.

The ladybug, a red beetle that feeds on soft insects, is an aid to agriculture. Its red color is associated with beneficial fire. Its origin is said to be supernatural, and its German name, *Marienkäfer* (Mary's Insect), denotes its connection with the Virgin Mary. It is a sign of good fortune, but it must be allowed to fly away of its own accord (*Standard Dictionary of Folklore, Mythology and Legend,* Funk and Wagnalls, p. 289). It is a helpful feminine instinct that operates best if unimpeded by the intervention of consciousness.

A herald was an officer whose business it was to proclaim war or peace; a messenger or forerunner who was invested with a sacred and inviolable character; reminiscent of Hermes, the messenger of the gods. Here he is a harbinger of peace since he is trying to communicate the way for the two sides to contact each other.

Developments seem to be going well in the unconscious feminine side. In his masculine consciousness, however, the patient is still struggling. The blue dwarf, his alter ego, now has a direction but is still unsure about how to achieve his goal.

The dolphins, representatives of the guiding, saving, instinctual intelligence, are in the water now, where they belong, guarding the still lethargic part of the patient.

Connecting everything together once again is the red string of connectedness, relatedness and feeling, up one end of which climbs a baboon.

The baboon might suggest the "Ape of God," the instinctual

aspect of the spirit, which is on the most direct line to the chalice. And it might well be that the life of the instincts was a first step toward wholeness and the spirit for this patient.

Another possibility that suggests itself regarding the baboon is Thoth, the Egyptian god of wisdom and learning. Thoth, whose symbol was the baboon, was self-begotten and the creator of speech. As a searcher for truth, he retrieved the eye of Ra, the sun god, and as a reward Ra created the moon for him, or gave Thoth the power to create it. As lord of the moon and the night sky, Thoth was the measurer of time and later became the god of magic, medicine and healing. Thoth officiated at the judgment of the dead, when a man's heart must be weighed against the feather of truth.

Climbing the red thread that the patient called the most direct way to the goal, the baboon might represent here the patient's own nascent moon-feminine consciousness, his own instinctual potentiality for healing, wisdom and truth.

The baboon's (instinct's) efforts to climb into the picture, and the peasants working on the earth in the diagonally opposite corner (where earlier there had been threatening snakes) appear to be positive developments. But the patient's tendencies toward passivity and unconsciousness remain, as indicated by the dozing Mexican who floats inappropriately and even dangerously on the water. One wonders whether the dolphins could guide or carry him unless he awakens. Perhaps they are trying to wake him up.

The patient's feeling about the skull behind the mirror in the lower right-hand corner was negative. However his comment regarding the skull was an indication of a burgeoning consciousness when he said, "The crusaders are not in touch with the negative aspects of their life on the little hill. Perhaps they are too self-involved, their vision of life may be too narrow."

The last few pictures have revealed various degrees of differentiation between the masculine and feminine aspects of the personality. This picture, and those that follow, manifest an integrative process of the masculine and feminine, a potentiality for union.

The specific early indications of integration in this picture are: the patient's statement that questing males on the right are seeking to reach the feminine; the blue dwarf's receptivity and longing to cross over; the herald's attempt to communicate instructions for the crossing, the half-finished bridge and the sign that gives incomprehensible instructions; and the red string of connection that extends from the struggling baboon to the feminine chalice, and that is the most difficult but direct route.

PICTURE 11

Description

The center of the picture consists of an elevated rectangular earth formation that has been hollowed out. On the left end stands a large circular mirror. Three polished stones are within the formation, and four are on the walls, totaling seven stones. On the lower left edge of the formation is perched a miniature silver sailing ship with a man at the tiller. To the right in the hollowed-out area is a round mirror-lake with a fire at its center. The "silver" elephant sits on the shore contemplating the scene. The blue dwarf stands above. At the upper left corner stands a figure of Buddha. In the lower left corner, the African phallic god. In the lower right corner a totem.

Patient's Comments

(The patient was silent while making this picture and through most of the hour.) Finally, he said:

This is an extinct volcano. In it is a crater-lake. The whole thing is a shrine, like Stonehenge or something. I used the mirror for the

11. Fire on the Water

lake because crater-lakes are so clear. There is a fire on the water. It is a magical place.
The silver boat has ridden on the wind. It is associated with searching, wandering souls. It has landed now.
I love the blue dwarf's sense of wonder.
Somewhere, something is observing all this, that's the mirror.

(The patient seemed quite moved. After a long silence he spoke:

Look, the sand is popping and moving. Maybe it's a young mountain, like the Rockies where things are always moving. (Again a long silence.)

Observations

The sand was indeed popping and moving. I had never noticed the phenomenon before. After watching together for a while, the patient suggested that it might be caused by the drying of the sand. We sat quietly together for most of the hour.

The picture did have a magical quality: the seven stones and the coming together of the opposites, fire and water; especially the appearance of fire for the first time, suggesting that the patient was experiencing feeling at a deeper level than he ever had before.

Seven, the number of stones in the picture, has been a mystical number historically—the seven heavenly spheres, the seven astrological planets, the seven notes of a music scale, the seven cardinal sins and virtues, etc.

Seven is the sum of three and four. Three implies the unification or reconciliation of opposites; thesis, antithesis, synthesis. It is a dynamic number that results from the tension of opposites. It is the mean between two numbers, resolving the tension between any two numbers. In that sense it is a reconciling symbol that resolves a conflicted state, implying a new beginning. Three refers to three-dimensional reality and is therefore an ego number since the ego exists in finite real time. Jung refers to three as a metaphor for the process of development in time. He states that the third dimension (depth) adds reality, and solidity to what would otherwise be a two-dimensional plane (*CW,* Vol. 2, pp. 180ff.).

In *Ego and Archetype* (pp. 179ff.; p. 184), Edinger refers to the number three as masculine and active. It is a number denoting process, a dynamic whole. Four, the number of wholeness, is the goal and therefore would be a structural whole. It is a containing image and therefore feminine. On that basis the number seven would then also be a union of the masculine and feminine.

The patient's remarking on the wonderment of the blue dwarf was a projection, I felt, of his own feeling of awe. When he spoke of something "observing all" he seemed to be reflecting his own sense of a suprapersonal power.

In the context of this picture, the landing of the airborne, silver, seagoing ship might signify the coming down to earth, finally, of the misguided spiritual quest. A man at the tiller suggests a guiding human consciousness or ego. To be sure, the boat has not yet reached the water where it belongs. Perhaps that will be possible when the fire melts the glacial crater lake that exists somewhere still in the patient.

PICTURE 12

Description

Two narrow streams of water meet and merge into a larger stream.

In the upper right-hand corner is a "silver" elephant; nearby lies a beached carp; three Chinese wisemen stand near a beached canoe. In the lower right-hand quadrant, a man carrying balancing scales has crossed a bridge over a narrow stream.

An owl sits on the sand in the lower center.

In the center of the picture, a mirror represents a well, a bridge supports a temple and a skull is nearby.

In the lower left-hand quadrant is another "silver" elephant. Two cranes are by the water near a black African medicine man. Across the stream stands a male Chinese pilgrim with a staff.

In the upper left-hand quadrant a pagoda is perched halfway up the mountain. On top of the mountain stands an African goddess effigy. Behind the goddess on a lower level is the green egg. In the upper left-hand corner are the figures of a man with his arm around a boy.

A red string marks the perimeter of the picture.

Patient's Comments

The carp came right up from the depths. The three Chinese wisemen don't even see it.

The elephants are male and female and they are calling across to each other, back and forth down the valley.

The man with the scales is just going ahead with his business.

The Chinese pilgrim is still trying but he is not getting very far.

The cranes are disinterested.

The African medicine man is doing an incantation to his totem on the mountain.

The mirror is the central well. It's where the energy is. The bridge is supporting a temple of life. But the skull warns that it is dangerous to attempt too much.

The red string contains and connects everything.

The man is a worker walking with his son. He has walked this path every day. The son keeps asking questions. The father has no answers. He had longed for the egg and the totem, but he didn't know how to get to them really. Now he recognizes it's beyond his reach. The son will have to find his own way.

12. The Son Will Find His Way

Observations

After a brief attempt at a reconciliation, the patient and his woman friend finally parted. He had a dream in which he saw her and was tempted to go after her, but decided against it, feeling sad, empty and resigned, which was a fair reflection of how he was feeling when he made this picture. He was anxious also about his approaching departure.

The patient's somewhat depressed state is reflected by the three Chinese wisemen who do not see the carp that is available for the taking. Yet the carp is an important fresh-water food fish in Asia. It is known for its endurance and perseverance. Like the salmon it struggles upstream. It can live out of the water for a considerable length of time. Here nourishment from the unconscious arrives "miraculously," and no one notices.

The cranes, which are land, air, and water birds, are generally seen as psychopomps and symbols for justice, loyalty and diligence. They were sacred to Artemis, Athene, Apollo and Hermes. Here they are indifferent.

The Chinese pilgrim makes no headway.

The pagoda seems abandoned in the bleak landscape, as does the green egg.

Despite the patient's saddened state, there are positive elements in this picture:

The elephants trumpet energetically to each other, indicating that the patient's instinctual energies are alive and well.

The mirror-well of energy is at the center. It contains much of the energy and symbolizes here, I believe, the unconscious. It supports a temple of life, although ignored.

The skull, lying not far from where a plane once crashed (Pictures 2 and 8), reminds one of the danger of inflated ambition, indicating a new consciousness in the patient.

In the upper left-hand corner—where snakes had once lain (Picture 9) and where Chinese peasants later worked the earth

(Picture 10)—now a western working man walks with his arm around his son, admitting that his former ways of questing failed and that now the young son (the reborn ego) must find a new individual way.

The father and son vignette indicates several developments: readiness for further resolution of the father complex, separation from and reconciliation with the father and his own punitive superego, the end of the inflationary sense of superiority and noblesse oblige (the father is an ordinary woodsman). Indicated, too, is a new relationship between the patient and the young aspect of himself. Depression and unconsciousness is apparent, for the egg, which had been in a high mountain crater previously (Picture 7), is now accessible, but the woodsman does not realize it.

The goddess on the mountain is at the same location as the crystal chalice had been, indicating a descent to a more primitive and instinctual level of the psyche.

The owl, which can be both positive and negative, seems ambiguous in this picture, as in earlier ones.

In the lower right-hand corner, where it was speculated the baboon Thoth had struggled to enter the sand tray (Picture 10), a man carrying balance scales has entered and made a crossing. Thoth, it will be remembered, was the Egyptian god of wisdom and justice, who presided over the weighing of hearts in the underworld, where a pure heart must balance against a feather representing truth.

Here the man balances the balance scales on his shoulder, perhaps reflecting a new possibility for psychological equilibrium in the patient.

The red string "contains everything, connects it all." One is reminded of the Tibetan meditation of the inner fire wherein a red thread is said to melt the intellect.

Lastly, the entire picture stands on a landscape where two streams have joined.

PICTURE 13

Description

A design in the sand with a hill in the center.

In the upper corners stand the two "silver" elephants. On the right stands a crescent shape. At the center of the top boundary is propped an adobe disc, marked into six sections. Below it stands a barren tree with a gold colored ring in its branches.

In the approximate center of the hill is a polished black stone. At the base of the tree and on either side of the black stone are colored enamel coppers in rough triangular shapes.

Below the center stands the blue dwarf looking into a round mirror.

Behind him at the bottom margin of the tray stands a midget Viking, no doubt his shadow.

On the left side stands an adobe cone in a circular space; below it a polished mineral stone. On the right side stands a miniature blue bottle, also in a circular space, and below it a translucent mineral stone, also difficult to discern.

A red string extending from a hole in the adobe hut spirals around the hill in the center of the picture.

Patient's Comments

I was just fooling around and then I suddenly saw a pattern emerge. The whole figure in the sand is a scarab.

The tree is a natural totem. It's not dead, just dormant. The two elephants are calling across to each other again and the energy is holding the golden ring in the tree. The blue dwarf, who is sometimes sleepy, is wide awake now and looking at himself in the mirror, the eye of the scarab. It's kind of a self-discovery.

The Norse midget is on his way somewhere. He is behind the dwarf.

The adobe hut is protection. One could look up at the tree through the hole.

I put the string in the hole of the hut just to connect things up.

The red string is partly aesthetic, to get a swirling effect, pulling everything together.

I put the blue bottle there as a balance. It seemed to fit and I liked the color.

I chose the adobe disc because it looked like a zodiac, except it only has six sections. The crescent is kind of a moon, I guess.

Observations

The patient was feeling somewhat better now, a week later, but still sad about the end of his relationship and suffering other separation pangs. He was somewhat anxious about his new job and the prospects of establishing a new life. His sadness and anxiety were alleviated by the flurry of activity required in his preparation for his departure which was only a month away.

With all the inner and outer activity, the process in the sand tray continued.

The balancing dynamics hinted at by the man with the scales is here developed more fully. With the exception of the crescent moon on the right, the picture is balanced.

The scarab is a beetle that pushes a ball of dung in which it has laid its eggs. Therefore, the ancient Egyptians conceived of it as being born out of its own substance, and it became a symbol for the self-generating, self-renewing aspect of the sun god Ra. Khepri, the name of the god of the rising sun, means both "he who comes into existence" and "scarab." Khepri was represented either as a scarab-headed man or as a scarab pushing the disc of the new sun (Ions, p. 46).

The scarab symbolized the renewal of life and eternal extistence.

In the context of this scarab picture, it may not be assuming too much to see the adobe disc with its radiating lines and made of clay, water and sunlight, as analogous to the rising mythological Egyptian solar disc.

13. A Scarab

The implication that a new consciousness or dynamism may be readying itself in the primordial layers of the unconscious is supported by the number of groupings of three in the picture. There are three enameled copper triangles, three polished mineral stones, three circular forms (the golden ring and the two circular spaces on either side of it). The gold ring in this context can be seen as a third eye, as can the adobe sun disc. The disc has six rays—twice three. There are three ridges below and above the scarab's body.

Looking at the picture from another prospective, one can see in it the eyes of an owl and the eyes are composed of feminine vessels, the adobe hut and the blue bottle. Beside it is the feminine crescent moon. Here again is the implication of a change toward feminine consciousness.

The owl can see and move swiftly and silently in darkness and in the light. It has both the positive and negative aspects of intuition. When related to life and reality it is positive; when not, it can be psychologically dangerous as any contents in the dark unconscious can be, if not related to external reality.

The owl, whose significance has been ambiguous in this series, now, with the intimation of a new consciousness, takes on a positive aspect.

It may be no accident that the owl, whose senses are so keen, becomes a positive symbol in the same picture where there are five circles (the solar adobe disc, the golden ring, the eyes of the owl, and the circular mirror); five being the number of sensation and the anthropos.

PICTURE 14

Description

This is the last picture. The patient called it "the celebration of a birth."

The body and wings of an eagle rise out of the water. Three polished stones delineate the eyes and mouth on the head. High on the shoulders stand two totems.

Below them the blue dwarf stands gazing across a fire at a blonde, female blue dwarf, who looks across at him. (The fire is discernible in pictures 14A.) Behind her stands a circular mirror.

On the lower left wing is a black African tribal drummer. At the left center, in the angle where the wing meets the body, the dozing Mexican lies on some moss. Below the moss, a bridge connects the left wing and the body. Below that, where the earth meets the water, stands a crane. At the lower left corner is a female "silver" elephant.

Below the blue dwarf, at the center of the picture, is a revolving merry-go-round to which is attached the African totem (now called a god by the patient). Below the totem lies a child before whom two nuns kneel.

On the right wing, near the shoulder, a military bugler plays his instrument. Midway down the wing, near the water, stands another crane. Further on are two sheep. At the lowest point, at the right, stands the male "silver" elephant.

A bridge connects the right wing and the body. Below the bridge are some moss and a frog.

At the base of the picture, at the center of the lower boundary, stands a second mirror facing inward.

Once again the red string acts as a connector.

Patient's Comments

It's the celebration of a birth! It's a birth scene.

It started as an eagle in the earth. I saw it in the sand as I was messing around to see what I could see.

14. A Celebration

14 a.

Our favorite dwarf is meeting a woman and there's a fire between them. The fire is warming and cleansing and purifying, but it's also a barrier, an obstacle to a full encounter. After all, a fire can burn. Maybe the obstacle is part of the path.

I put in the mirror because I wanted him to be able to see what he was doing.

I'm not sure why I put in the cranes. I just like them.

The animals and people have come together and are making music because it's a celebration. The male elephant on the right is more excited, less controlled than the female on the left. They're both trumpeting, but the male is a little looser. He's letting out all the stops. He had been the controlled one. The frog near him is singing along in a very deep voice.

The laid-back Mexican is taking it all in. Relaxed, trusting, letting it happen.

The nuns and the babe are a touch of the traditional.
The military bugler is a smaller part, but he is not to be denied.
I put the sheep on the male side more for balance.
The bridges felt like triumphal arches. They fit the celebration, they hook everything up.
The string connects everything in a circuitous way. There's a lot of color.
The carousel is the symbol of life. It makes and uses energy. It's an essential life force at the center, unplanned. The god is hooked to the carousel. God came from the carousel; coalesced out of it. Or maybe it's the other way around, the carousel came from God.
The mirror at the base is like an eye from the outside, a gateway as well.

Observations

He spoke with great intensity, excitement and joy.

I continued scribbling after he stopped speaking as he sat quietly waiting for me to finish. After a moment or two, I looked up and saw him smiling with filled eyes. So we just sat for a while. The groupings of three that emerged in the last picture are reiterated here: three totems, two nuns and the baby, the two dwarfs and the fire, all betokening a very powerful dynamism.

There are two new developments: the emergence of the anima, the image of his own psychological feminine aspect; and the fire that relates the nascent masculine ego with the anima is in the heart region, where it belongs. Perhaps the placement of the mirror behind the female is to provide not only consciousness of the ego's activity, but of the unseen shadow side of the man's inner feminine nature.

The yoking of the primitive divine figure to the circular "life force" implies the activation of the Self.

Totems are representations of tribal membership, of feelings of belonging to a group. Here the appearance of the three totems may signify a changing attitude, which might be signaling the end—at least potentially—of the patient's lifelong feeling of emotional isolation.

The eagle was the bird or emblem of Zeus. Its appearance here reminds one of the earlier appearance of the face of Zeus (Picture 9). The eagle represents masculine energy of great natural strength. Here, rising out of maternal watery unconscious, we see the beginnings of an instinctual, masculine consciousness that is native to this man's own personality and quite distinct from the earlier patriarchal identification derived from his father complex.

The figures representing the ego and the anima are dwarfs, symbolic of the wonder-workers of the great goddess. They are primitive elements operating deep in the matriarchal level, or perhaps in what E.C. Whitmont (*The Symbolic Quest,* p. 270) has called "the magical dimension." They are only partially human.

However, the new infant before whom the nuns kneel indicates that the "life force" evolutionary process already in motion has in readiness a human/divine development. It may well be that the celebration is to commemorate a resurrection and the birth of a new life, at least in potentia.

A mirror is a symbol of the unconscious as it reflects back to us that which we have not seen; as such it represents an impulse toward consciousness, a potential capacity to disidentify with unconscious contents. Edinger (1975, p. 35) suggests that "meditative reflection can turn an oppressive mood into an object of knowledge by discovering the meaningful image imbedded in the mood." The image may be too dangerous to look at directly. It was via Athena's mirror-shield that Perseus could safely see and slay Medusa.

The mirror that stands behind the anima figure in this picture, into which the blue dwarf looks, is perhaps an image of the personal unconscious and the urge to gain further ego consciousness, to "know."

Edinger suggests further that consciousness requires the experience of the ego as knowing subject *plus* the experience of being the known object, of being the object of knowledge with the function of the knowing subject residing in the "other." He goes on to say that "The archetypal image that carries the clearest symbolic expressions of the ego's experience of being the known object is the image of the Eye of God" (p. 35).

The patient's comments regarding the large mirror at the base of the picture suggest it represents the Eye of God or the Self.[1]

On the basis of these ideas it is possible to infer that in this last picture the experiences required for consciousness, the ego as knowing subject and as known object are here implied, at least as potentialities.

It is interesting that the news cameraman in Picture 2 who represented perhaps a new objectivity in the search for meaning was in the same position in the sand tray as is now the Eye of God, the transpersonal observer who observes all, including the nascent ego figure represented by the blue dwarf.

Edinger (1975, p. 42) suggests that in psychological terms the eye (Shiva's third eye, the eye of Ra, the watchful eye of Horus) "will be destructive of all in the ego that is not appropriately related to the Self."

Since the eye in this picture seems benign, perhaps it indicates the resolution of the inflationary ego-Self identity from which the patient had suffered.

As the picture was being dismantled, an interesting image emerged. The red string that the patient insisted "connects everything" seemed to outline the body of a woman in a red gown, superimposed on the great eagle; a kind of instinctive

---

[1]In *Ego and Archetype,* Edinger expresses the analogy to the Self elegantly when he says, "The image of the Eye of God suggests a unified consciousness (vision) within the unconscious" (Edinger, 1972, p. 284).

union of opposites of Logos and Eros, that underlay the whole picture.

There is no real greenery in this last picture of the series, just some moss down by the water, indicating that the process is unfinished and at a very early stage, perhaps a first major step.

The final meeting, a double session, occurred two weeks later when the slide series was shown and discussed. I wondered at the time whether the case was not too neat. Although the dreams had confirmed the process, it was possible that the patient manipulated the pictures to please me. The anima appearing just in time for his departure seemed too good to be true. At the moment that these thoughts were occurring, the patient reported a dream he had had a few days *after* making the last picture:

I met a new woman at a social gathering. She was very attractive although her features were not distinct. I called her and we went out once or twice. I became very attracted and she was too, but I didn't want to move too fast. I was thinking of our living together, family, and all that. Others, my friends, were suggesting that she was the one for me and that I should pursue her harder. I felt I was moving at the right pace and that we were very comfortable and happy with the way things were going.

There was a lot more to the dream which I don't remember, but overall it had a very positive feeling. Content and whole.

Needless to say, the dream was reassuring.

Although the patient's sandplay therapy was interrupted in this still very early stage, significant growth and real change had taken place:

- The father complex was largely resolved, as was the identification with the intellect.
- There was a period of intense confusion with the emergence of the sensation/reality function and the previously repressed feeling.

- The incipient paranoid delusional system and the dangerous inflation were arrested, as was the crippling obsessive compulsivity.
- Differentiation of masculine and feminine functioning occurred.
- As his own feelings evolved, he withdrew the anima projection from his woman friend, and found that he could love her. But she was apparently unable to adjust to the loss of control of the relationship and so it foundered.
- He changed his lifestyle and left his therapy with feelings of buoyancy and optimism, mixed with sadness and some anxiety.

Whether or not these developments occurred solely as a result of sandplay is impossible to determine. Prior to the introduction of sandplay, however, the patient had made little or no progress in his verbal analysis, since any insight that even remotely challenged his ego-Self identification was rejected out of hand. Therefore, it is reasonable to believe that sandplay therapy expedited penetration of his resistance and achieved its primary goal of reaching the transpersonal level of the personality and successfully strengthening the ego.

As we can see repeatedly, this non-verbal, non-rational therapy functions effectively as an autonomous process; as an adjunct to the analytical work it activates, accelerates and facilitates the therapeutic process. At this point in time, the importance and far reaching significance of sandplay is yet to be fully realized. Further practice and research will certainly develop both the clinical use of sandplay and its literature. It is my personal hope that IMAGES OF THE SELF will stimulate wider and deeper interest in this valuable psychotherapeutic process.

GLOSSARY

Active imagination—A method of deliberately and actively fantasizing. Usually the ego engages in an imaginary dialogue or action with an imaginary figure that represents a personified aspect of that individual's psyche. A powerful tool that can activate uncontrollable unconscious contents, active imagination should be used with caution, particularly if the ego is unstable. In Jung's words (*CW* 14, p. 495, par. 706), "You choose a dream or some other fantasy image and concentrate on it by simply catching hold of it and looking at it. You can also use a bad mood as a starting point and then try to find out what sort of fantasy image it will produce, or what image expresses this mood. You then fix this image in the mind by concentrating your attention. Usually, it will alter as the mere fact of contemplating it animates it. The activations must be carefully noted down all the time, for they reflect the psychic processes in the unconscious background, which appear in the form of images consisting of conscious memory material. In this way, conscious and unconscious are united."

Anima and animus—The *anima* is the psychic personification of the feminine principle in men, the eros principle representing the capacity for connection, relatedness and love. A weak ego tends to identify with the anima. The man then becomes quite moody, unreliable and overly sensitive. The *animus* is the equivalent personification of the masculine principle in women. Its positive aspect reflects the masculine logos principle, the capacity for consciousness and logical thinking. If the feminine ego is weak, it identifies with the animus and results in rigid opinions and a power drive in the woman (*CW* 18, p. 73).

Archetypal image of the mother—We all carry deep in the unconscious an archetypally determined image of a nurturing mother that represents our archetypal need and predisposition for experiencing the nurturing mother. When mothering has, for one reason or another, been inadequate, the image of mother emerges as malignant rather than beneficent, and one speaks of an "injured" mother imago. This "injured" image can adversely affect the development of the personality, giving rise to a whole gamut of neuroses and psychoses unless or until a more positive corrective experience can modify it.

Archetypes—Archetypes are to the psyche what instincts are to the body. As with instincts, the existence of archetypes can only be inferred by the effects they produce (Edinger, 1968). Archetypes are innate psychic dynamisms, universal predispositions toward typical forms of human apprehension and emotional and behavioral responses to experience. Experience is translated into inner images or impressions that are influenced by both the archetype and the individual's subjective response to the experience. These representations or images in turn affect our responses and behavior. We can infer from this hypothesis that changes in an image will bring about changes in response.

Cathexis—A Freudian term. "The investment of the libido on an object, another person or the self. The concentration of mental energy on an emotion, idea or line of action, giving the object (emotion, idea, action or personality) significance or importance" (Chaplin, 1968). *Decathexis* is the withdrawal of that libido from the object back to the subject.

Compensation—Implies that there is a relationship between the unconscious and the conscious mind wherein a content missing from consciousness and required for wholeness of the personality will appear in an accentuated form in the unconscious, making itself known through a dream or a powerful affect deriving from an activated complex.

Complex—The core of a complex is an archetype or an archetypal image that constellates related ideas and associations derived from personal experience. An activated complex induces strong emotional responses and disturbs normal functioning of the ego.

Constellate—The clustering of related unconscious contents (images, feelings) around an archetypal core, creating a psychic entity or gestalt, e.g., a complex, activation of the Self.

Counter-transference—(See Transference)

Dialogue with the unconscious—Since the unconscious is perceived as limitless, one of the aims of a Jungian analysis is to train the analysand to understand the symbolic meaning of his dreams and fantasies so that individuation and interaction with the unconscious become a lifelong discipline.

Ego—A complex of ideas which constitutes the center of an

individual's field of consciousness and appears to possess a high degree of continuity and identity. The ego is only the center of the field of consciousness. It is not identical with the totality of the psyche, being merely one complex among other complexes. The ego is only the subject of a person's consciousness, while the Self is the subject of the total psyche, which also includes the unconscious (*CW* 6, p. 425, par. 706).

Extraversion—An outward turning of libido, a positive movement of subjective interest toward the object, a transfer of interest from subject to object. It is active when intentional, and passive when the object compels it, i.e., when the object attracts the subject's interest of its own accord, even against his will. When extraversion is habitual, we speak of the extraverted type (*CW* 6, p. 427, par. 710).

Fantasy—According to Neumann (*The Child,* p. 144), "Human fantasy is not a regressively wishful function; rather, it is an anticipatory and preparatory form of adaptation to life. The fantasy of a transformed world is the first stage in its real transformation and must not be confused with regressive wishful thinking which characterizes neurotic flights from the world. The world of art . . . of culture and civilization with all its inventions, including the invention of science, springs from man's creative fantasy. What determines whether a man is sick or healthy is not the intensity of his fantasy life but his ability or inability to transform it into reality."

Feeling—One of the four basic functions (see *Functions*). According to Jung (*CW* 6, p. 434, par. 725), feeling is "a subjective process to set up a subjective criterion of acceptance or rejection. Valuation of feeling extends to every content of consciousness . . . when intensity of feeling increases, it turns into an *affect* (or emotion), i.e., a feeling state accompanied by marked physical innervations."

Functions—Functions are the habitual means by which we experience and evaluate the world and ourselves. Jung described four basic psychological functions: (1) sensation—sense perception of a fact; (2) thinking—finding objective meaning of the fact, classification, differentiation; (3) feeling—subjective evaluation of the fact; and (4) intuition—unconscious perception of the unseen potentialities of the fact.

Everyone has all four functions, although one or two may be more exercised and thus more developed than the others. We may therefore speak of a *thinking* type of person as different from a *feeling* type. For an innately feeling type to try to live as a thinking type (or vice versa) is to be as psychologically handicapped as a right-handed person would be physically handicapped by trying to function as if left-handed.

Gestalt—A structure or system of phenomena, whether physical, biological or psychological, so integrated as to constitute a functional unit with properties not derivable from its parts or some of those parts (Webster, 1958).

Identification—The subject is alienated from himself for the sake of the object in which he is disguised, according to Jung (*CW* 6, p. 440, par. 738). Identification is unconscious imitation. Imitation is conscious copying.

Identity—Denotes psychological conformity. Always unconscious. There is no separation between subject and object. Identity is a characteristic of the primitive mentality and the foundation for the participation mystique, which is a relic of the original nondifferentiation of subject and object and hence of the mental state of early infancy and the unconscious of the civilized adult (*CW* 6, pp. 440–441, pars. 741–742).

Image (Imago)—A psychic image consisting of both personal and archetypal (transpersonal) elements. According to Neumann (*Origins and History of Consciousness,* p. 401), "As the personal ties (of the child to the individual mother) grow stronger, the archetype is gradually replaced by the *imago,* in which personal and transpersonal characteristics are visibly blended and active."

Individuation—A developmental process of self-realization by which an individual is differentiated from the general psychology and from the complexes in his unconscious. In Jungian analysis, it is a dialectical process of interaction between the ego and the unconscious by which contents of the unconscious are brought into consciousness via analysis of dreams, fantasies and other products of the unconscious, thus enabling an individual to realize, not what he might like to be, but what he is. Since the unconscious is inexhaustible, it is not possible to achieve total self-realization or total consciousness; thus individuation is never complete. It is a way rather than a goal.

Inflation—According to Jung (*Memories, Dreams, Relfections,* p. 384), inflation is the "expansion of the personality beyond its proper limits by identification with the persona or with an archetype, or, in pathological cases, with a historical or religious figure. It produces an exaggerated sense of one's own self-importance and is usually compensated by feelings of inferiority."

Introversion—An inward turning of libido. Interest is withdrawn from the object into the subject. The subject is the prime motivating factor. The object is secondary. When introversion is habitual, we speak of the introverted type (*CW* 6, p. 452, par. 769).

Intuition—One of the four psychological functions (see *Functions*). It is the unconscious perception that perceives unseen possibilities of a given. The validity of an intuition should be checked by using the other functions, since intuitions are irrational and unconsciously determined and may be unconsciously colored by one's mood or an activated complex.

Libido—According to Edinger (*An Outline of Analytical Psychology*), libido is "the psychic energy that directs and motivates the personality. Interest, attention and drive are all expressions of libido. The libido invested in a given item is indicated by how highly that item is valued. Libido can be transformed or displaced, but not destroyed. If the libido attached to one object disappears, it reappears elsewhere."

Mandala—A universal archetypal image which consists, in its simplest form, of a circle within a square or a circle containing a square or a cross. It is a symbol of the Self, of order and integration. Mandalas appear in all cultures. According to Jung (*CW* 9, Part II, par. 60), "they occur in patients chiefly during times of psychic disorientation or reorientation. They depict or create order that transforms chaos into cosmos."

Matriarchal consciousness—The uroboric phase occurs in the prenatal and postnatal state, where there is no differentiation between inner and outer, subject or object (infant and mother), conscious and unconscious; no differentiation of ego from mother. The ego is identified with Self. In the later matriarchal phase, the nascent ego is still passive and identified with the mother. A very dim semiconsciousness begins to evolve.

Numinous—Derived from the word "numen" meaning the divine force or potency ascribed to objects or beings regarded with awe. The awe and awe-inspiring quality associated with religion, deity and the holy (Webster).

Persona—The psychic organ that mediates between the ego and the world, the mask that one assumes for roles one plays in society, or one's system of adaptation. If a person identifies with his persona, he loses connection to his true identity, which leads to a loss in psychological development. If the person is socially successful, identification with the persona leads to inflation and loss of realistic perception. If the person is socially unsuccessful, identification with the persona leads to self-devaluation and despair.

Projection—The process by which a person perceives an unconscious quality belonging to himself as belonging to another outer object or person. The projection can be positive or negative. Projections of animus or anima are experienced as falling in love. Withdrawal of projection makes possible a relationship with the reality of the other person.

Psychic image—According to Neumann (*The Child,* p. 153), "a psychic image of something in the world is both a deposit of experience and an organ of the psyche through which this image experiences and later interprets the world."

Self—The Self is the central archetype, and as such is transpersonal. As it manifests within the individual, the Self represents the totality of the personality, both consciousness and the unconscious. The Self is not identical with the ego, which is the psychological organ of consciousness. It is rather "an a priori existence out of which the ego evolves . . . an unconscious prefiguration of the ego" (*CW* 2, par. 391). Dynamically, the Self may be thought of as an innate drive toward wholeness. As an acorn to a particular oak tree, the Self carries the full, unique genetic endowment that needs to realize itself. Like an unconscious intelligence, if operating properly it acts as an organizing factor in the psyche that guides and supports psychological development.

Sensation—(See *Functions.*)

Shadow—This term is used to denote the personal unconscious—those attributes, both negative and positive, of which
the individual is unaware, and which can be made conscious
and integrated into the conscious personality. According to
Jung (*Memories, Dreams, Reflections,* p. 386), the shadow is
"the inferior part of the personality; the sum of all the personal
and collective psychic elements which, because of their incom-
patibility with the chosen conscious attitude, are denied expression in life and therefore coalesce into a relatively autonomous "splinter" personality with contrary tendencies in
the unconscious." The positive shadow consists of unknown
creative potentialities.

Superego—A Freudian term. That part of the psyche or personality which develops from the incorporation of moral
standards and prohibitions from the parents and particularly
the father that acts as an inhibitor of libidinal drives. It is
roughly equivalent to conscience (Chaplin, 1968).

Symbol—The best possible expression for something unknown. A symbol acts as a healing agent or bridge between
irreconcilable opposites, pointing the way to resolution of the
conflict. It arises spontaneously from the unconscious.

Synchronicity (or synchronistic event)—A term coined by
Jung to designate the meaningful coincidence arising out of an
acausal connecting principle, for example when an outer event
coincides with an inwardly perceived event (dream, vision,
premonition, etc.). The inner image or premonition has "come
true." Neither the one nor the other coincidence can be ex-
plained by causality. A synchronistic event produces awe and a
numinous feeling in the subject.

Thinking—(See *Functions*)

Transcendent function—According to Neumann (*Origins
and History of Consciousness,* p. 414), the transcendent function encompasses "the creative elements in the psyche which
can overcome a conflict situation not soluble to the conscious
mind, by discovering a new way, a new value or image . . . in
which the creativeness of the (unconscious) psyche and the
positiveness of the conscious mind no longer function like
two opposed systems split off from one another, but have
achieved a synthesis." This synthesis is often accompanied by

symbols of a *union of opposites,* for example, fire and water, or male and female images of the androgyne.

Transference/counter-transference—Projection of the analysand on the therapist, and the projection of the therapist on the patient.

Typology—(See *Functions*)

Union of Opposites—The libido or psychic energy that fuels and motivates human behavior is generated by the interaction and tension between opposing forces (drives and inhibitions) within the personality. The union of opposites "signifies the goal of individuation and the conscious realization of the Self" (Edinger, 1978, p. 148).

Uroborus—An archetypal circular image of a snake eating its own tail. A symbol of the original state of unconsciousness, of undifferentiated wholeness. No element is discretely realized, as when the infant is in a state of identifying with the mother and its ego exists only as a potentiality within the Self. Although physically separated from the mother, one might say that psychologically the infant is still in his own being. (See *Archetypal image of the mother.*)

BIBLIOGRAPHY

Aite, Paolo, "Ego and Image" in *Journal of Analytical Psychology*, October, 1978, Volume 23, No. 4.

Bowyer, Ruth, *Lowenfeld World Techniques*, Pergamon Press, New York, 1970.

Bradway, Katherine; Signell, Karen A.; Spare, Geraldine H.; Stewart, Charles T.; Stewart, Louis H.; Thompson, Clare. *Sandplay Studies: Origins, Theory and Practice*, C.G. Jung Institute, San Francisco 1981.

Chaplin, J.P. *Dictionary of Psychology*, Dell Publishing Co. N.Y.C. 1968.

Dundas, Evalyn, *Symbols Come Alive In The Sand*, Self-published, 1978.

Edinger, Edward, F. "An Outline of Analytical Psychology" in *Quadrant*, No. 1, C. G. Jung Foundation for Analytical Psychology, New York, 1968.

Edinger, Edward, F. *Ego and Archetype*, G. P. Putnam's Sons for C. G. Jung Foundation for Analytical Psychology, New York, 1972.

Edinger, Edward, F. "The Meaning of Consciousness" in *Quadrant*, Winter, 1975, Volume VIII, No. 2.

Edinger, Edward, F. *Melville's Moby Dick: A Jungian Commentary*. New Directions, New York 1978

Fordham, Michael C., "Active Imagination and Imaginative Activity" in *Journal of Analytical Psychology*, 1956, Volume I, Part 2.

Fordham, Michael C., *New Developments in Analytical Psychology*, Routledge, Kegan, Paul, London, 1957.

Fordham, Michael C., *Children As Individuals*, G.P. Putnam's Sons for C. G. Jung Foundation for Analytical Psychology, New York, 1970.

Funk & Wagnall's Standard Dictionary of Folklore, Mythology and Legend, Edited by Leach, M., New York, 1972.

Grolnick, S. A., Meunsterberger, W., et al, *Between Reality and Fantasy; Transitional Objects and Phenomena*, Jason Aronson, New York, 1978.

Harding, M. Esther, "What Makes The Symbol Effective As A Healing Agent" in *Current Trends In Analytical Psychology*, Edited by Gerhardt Adler, Tavistock Publications, London, 1961.

Harding, M. Esther, *The Parental Image; Its Injury and Reconstruction*, G. P. Putnam's Sons, New York, 1965.

Huizinga, Johann, *Homo Ludens; A Study of the Play Element In Culture*, translated by R. F. C. Hull, Beacon Press, Boston, 1955.

Ions, V., *Egyptian Mythology*, Hamlyn Publishing Group, Middlesex, Great Britain, 1968.

Jacobi, Jolande, *Complex/Archetype/Symbol in the Psychology of C.G. Jung*. Trans. by Ralph Manheim, Bollingen Series LVII, Princeton University Press, Princeton, 1959.

Jung, C.G. *The Collected Works of C.G. Jung*, Edited by Herbert Read, Michael Fordham, Gerhard Adler, William McGuire; translated by R.F.C. Hull; volumes 5, 6, 7, 8, 9I, 9II. Princeton (Bollingen Series XX) 1954.

Perera, Sylvia B., *Descent To The Goddess,* Inner City Books, Toronto, 1981.

Reed, Jeanette Pruyn, *Sand Magic,* J.P.R. Publishers, Albuquerque, New Mexico, 1975.

Reichard, Gladys A. *Navajo Religion; A Study of Symbolism,* Second Edition, Bollingen Series XVIII, Princeton University Press, Princeton, N.J., 1974.

Stein, Murray, "The Devouring Father" in *Fathers and Mothers, Spring Publications,* New York, 1973.

Stevens, Anthony, *Archetypes; A Natural History of The Self,* William Morrow & Co., Inc., New York, 1982.

Stewart, Louis H., "Sandplay Therapy: Jungian Technique." *International Encyclopedia of Psychiatry, Psychology, Psychoanalysis and Neurology,* 1977, Volume X, Aesculapius Publishers, New York, 1977.

Ulanov, Ann Belford, *The Feminine In Jungian Psychology and In Christian Theology,* Northwestern University Press, Evanston, 1971.

Webster's New International Dictionary, Second Edition, G. & C Merriam Co., Springfield, Mass., 1958.

Weinrib, E.L., "On Delayed Interpretation in Sandplay Therapy" in *Arms of the Windmill,* C.G. Jung Foundation, N.Y.C., 1983.

Whitmont, E.C., *The Symbolic Quest,* G.P. Putnam's Sons for C.G. Jung Foundation for Analytical Psychology, New York, 1969.

Winnicott, D.W., *The Maturational Processes and The Facilitating Environment,* International University Press, New York, 1965.

Winnicott, D.W., *Playing and Reality,* Basic Books, Incorporated, New York, 1971.

Winnicott, D.W., "Transitional Objects and Transitional Phenomena" in *Through Pediatrics To Psychoanalysis,* Basic Books, Incorporated, New York, 1975.

INDEX